AF254798

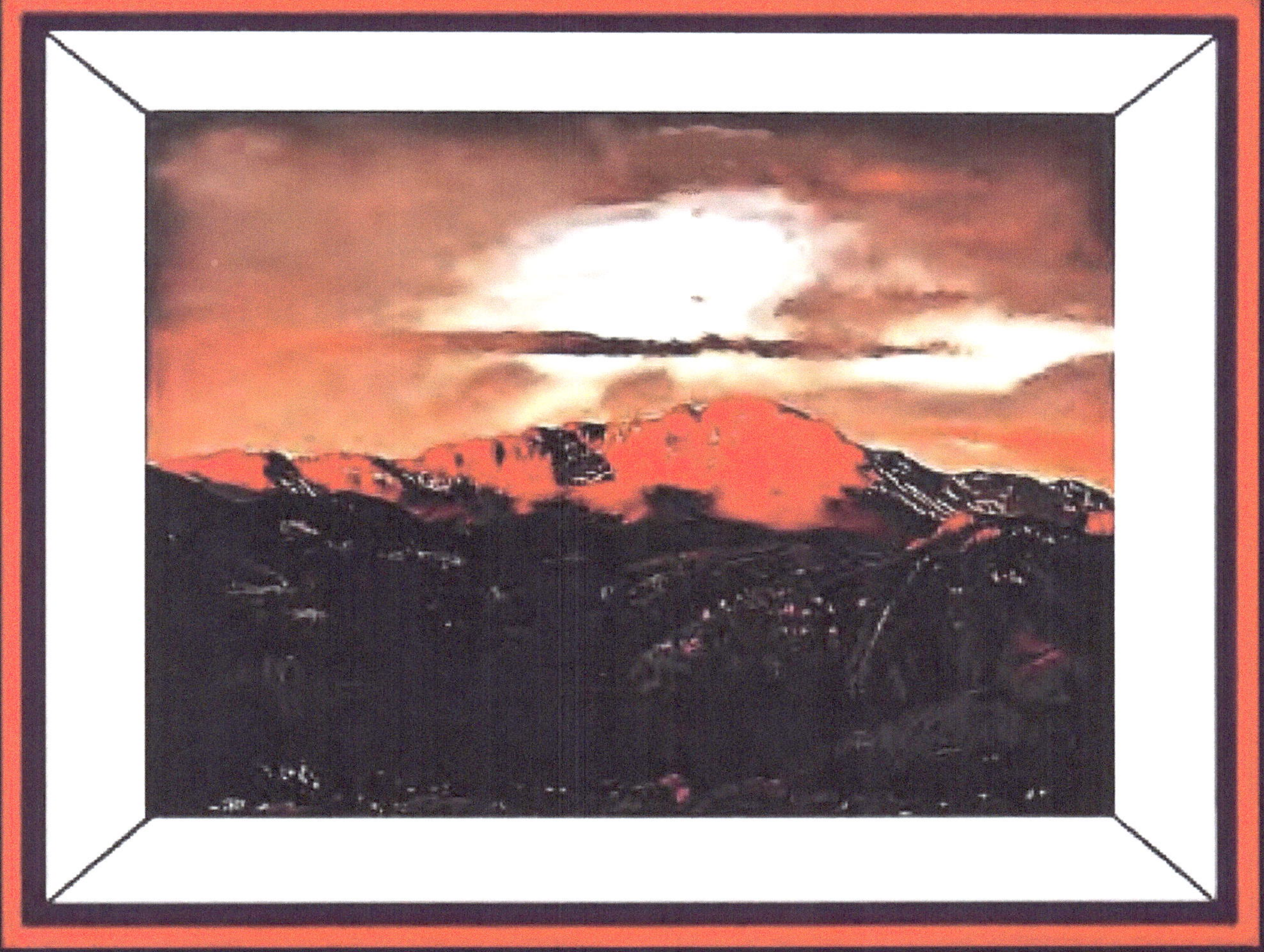

Destination:Pikes Peak

Backyard Observations
by Atwood Cutting

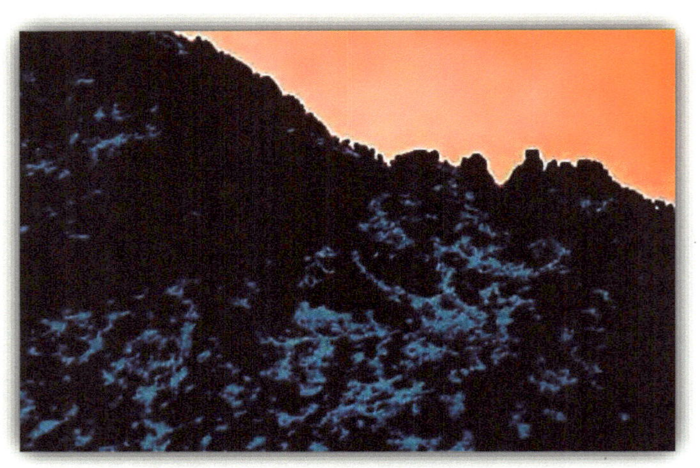

Destination:Pikes Peak

Backyard Observations by Atwood Cutting

ISBN: 978-0-578-29159-8
Copyright 2022: Echo Hill Arts Press
Colorado Springs, Colorado U.S.A.

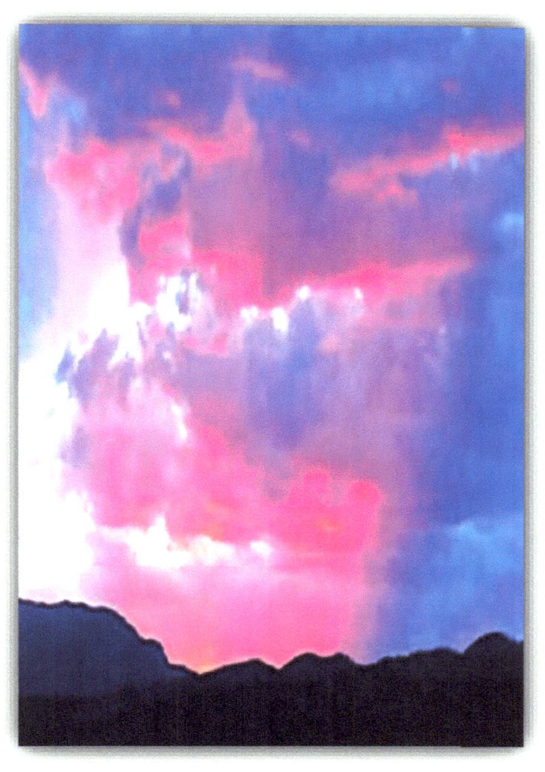

*Welcome to Colorado,
where skies overhead commonly project
a display of watercolor artistry.*

In 2012, we moved from the mild Midwest, to Colorado.

Just seven miles west of our new home in Colorado
Springs, Pikes Peak stood out as a monolith of pink granite
jutting up from the Rampart Range in the Rockies.

At an elevation of 14,115 feet, it is
the southernmost of Colorado's popular "Fourteeners."
A natural weather maker, its dominant bulk
protects the city from prevailing winds, and the crags
seem to reach up to snag the rain or snow-soaked clouds,
and hold them at bay.

Mesmerized by the way the sun played over the mountain
-particularly at dawn and dusk-
I quickly fell into a love affair with "America's Mountain."

In April of 2020, we moved back to the Heartland.
This book is my tribute to colorful Colorado,
to Pikes Peak, and to sunset skies over the Rockies.

I hope you will enjoy these views as much as we did.

Atwood Cutting

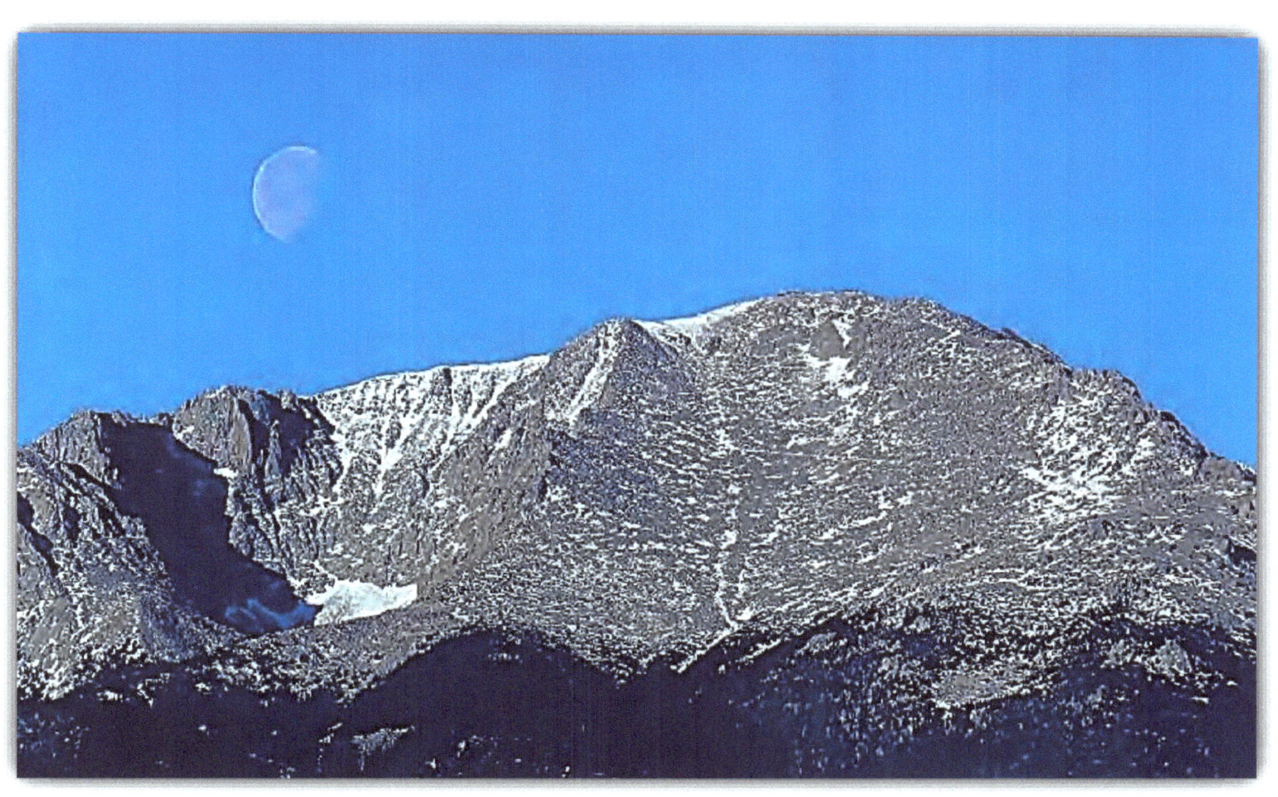

*Sitting out on the back deck with mugs
of morning coffee-watching the moon settle
down behind the mountain-this was our new
morning treat.*

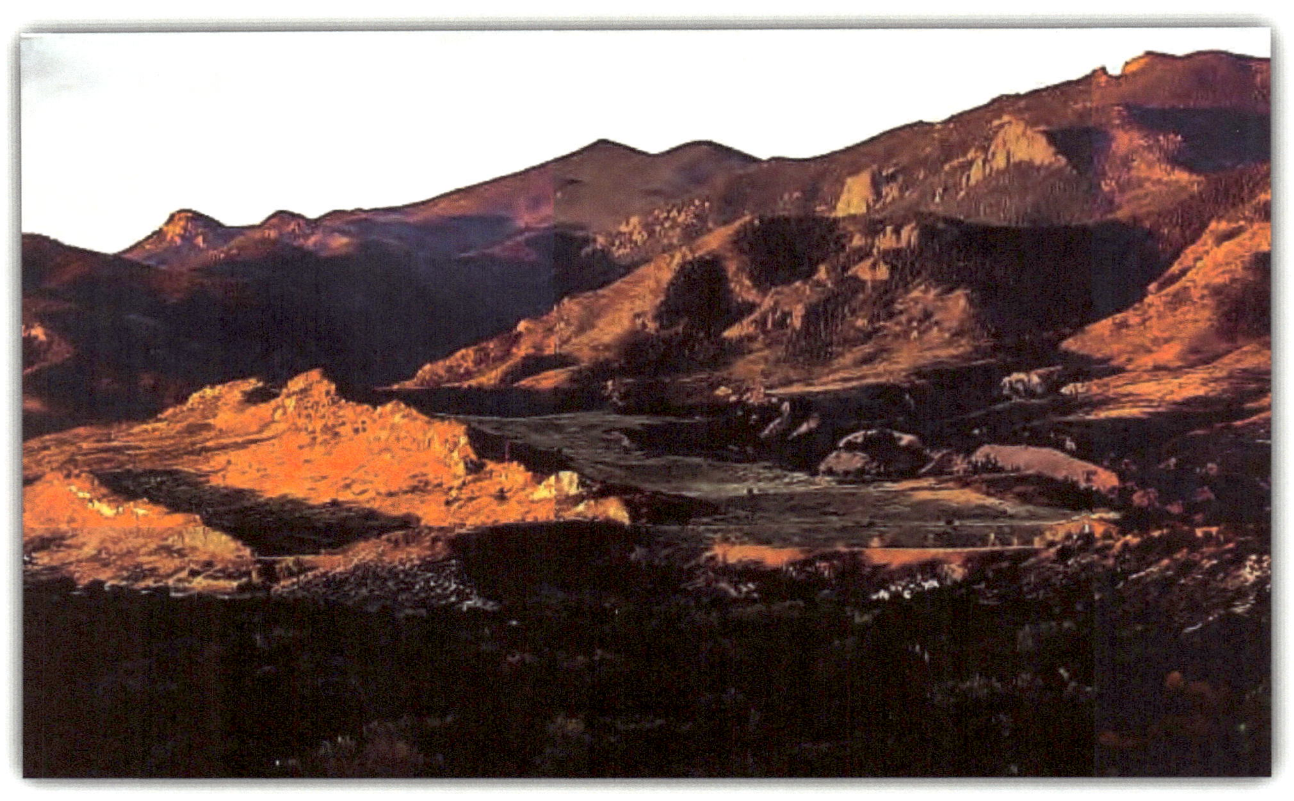

*As the sun peeked up over Cheyenne Mountain,
it highlighted the Front Range, where there was a big
open space that looked like a fun place to go sledding.*

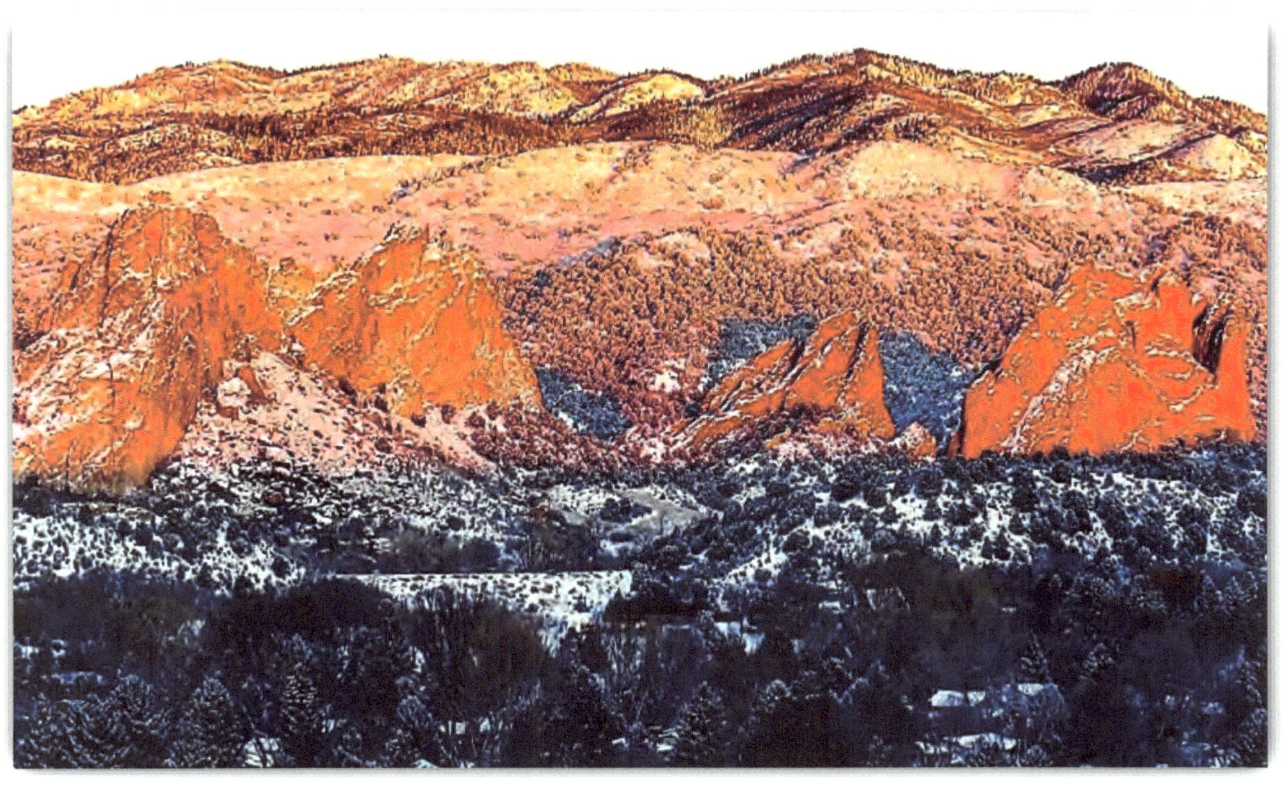

Then, dawn would illuminate Garden of the Gods,
making the giant red rocks glow.
Once the winter home of Native Americans,
it is now a very popular park.

*Some days, for a few fleeting moments
that first ray of sunlight will turn
the mountain a thrilling, iridescent
pink.*

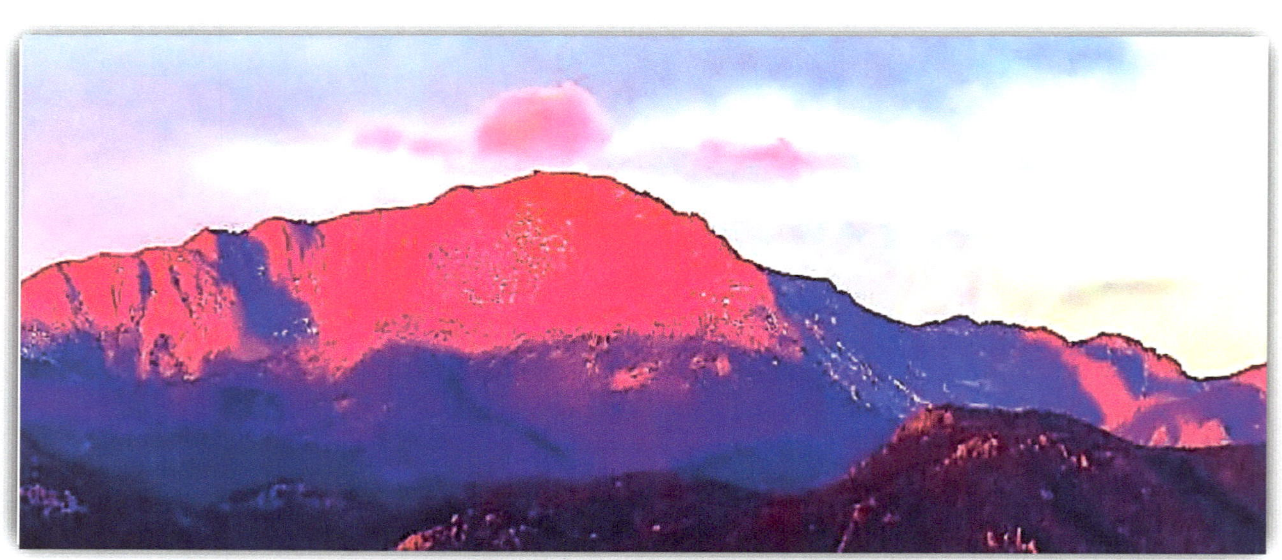

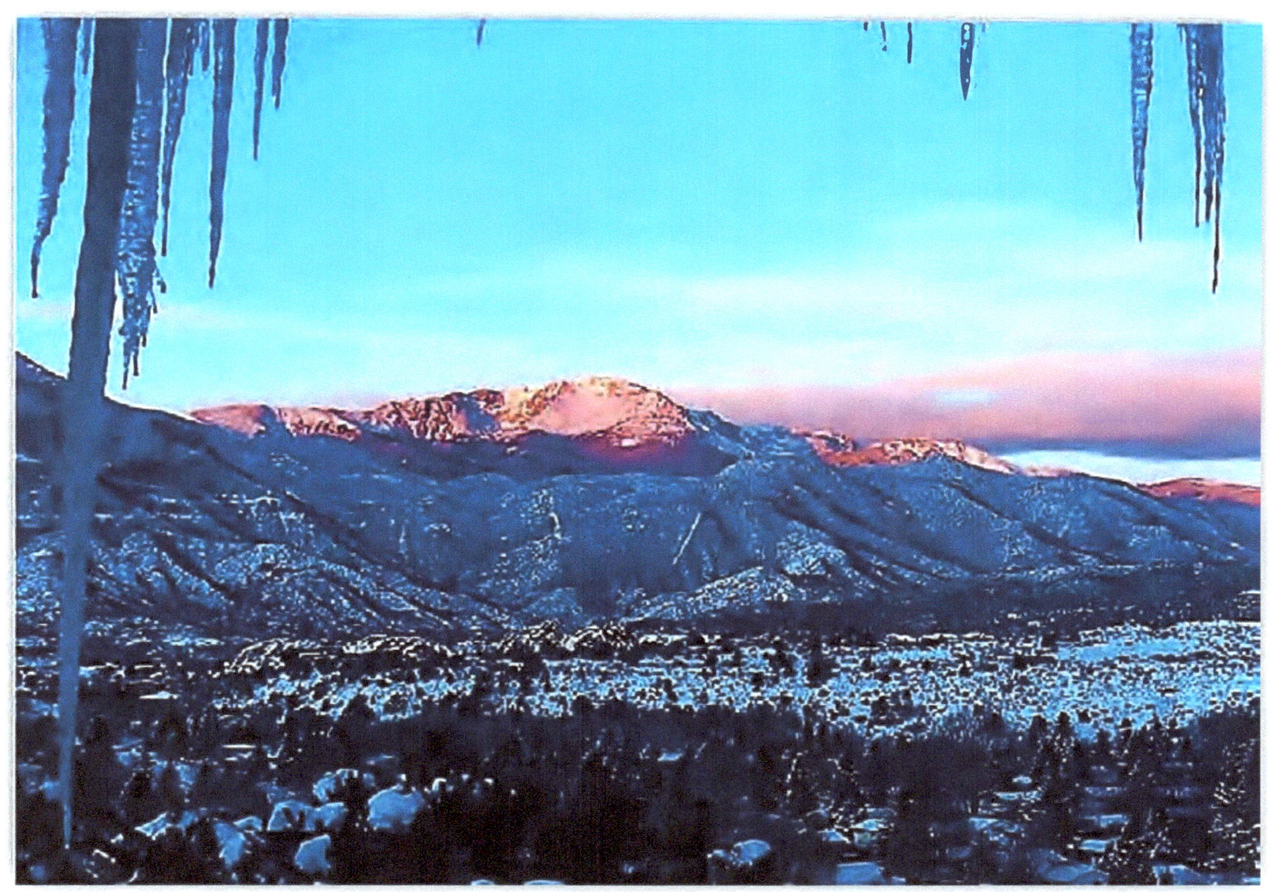

The white streak running uphill from Manitou Springs.
used to be a funicular amusement ride.
In 1990, it was re-purposed into a challenging stairway,
which Olympians and intrepid hikers like to climb.

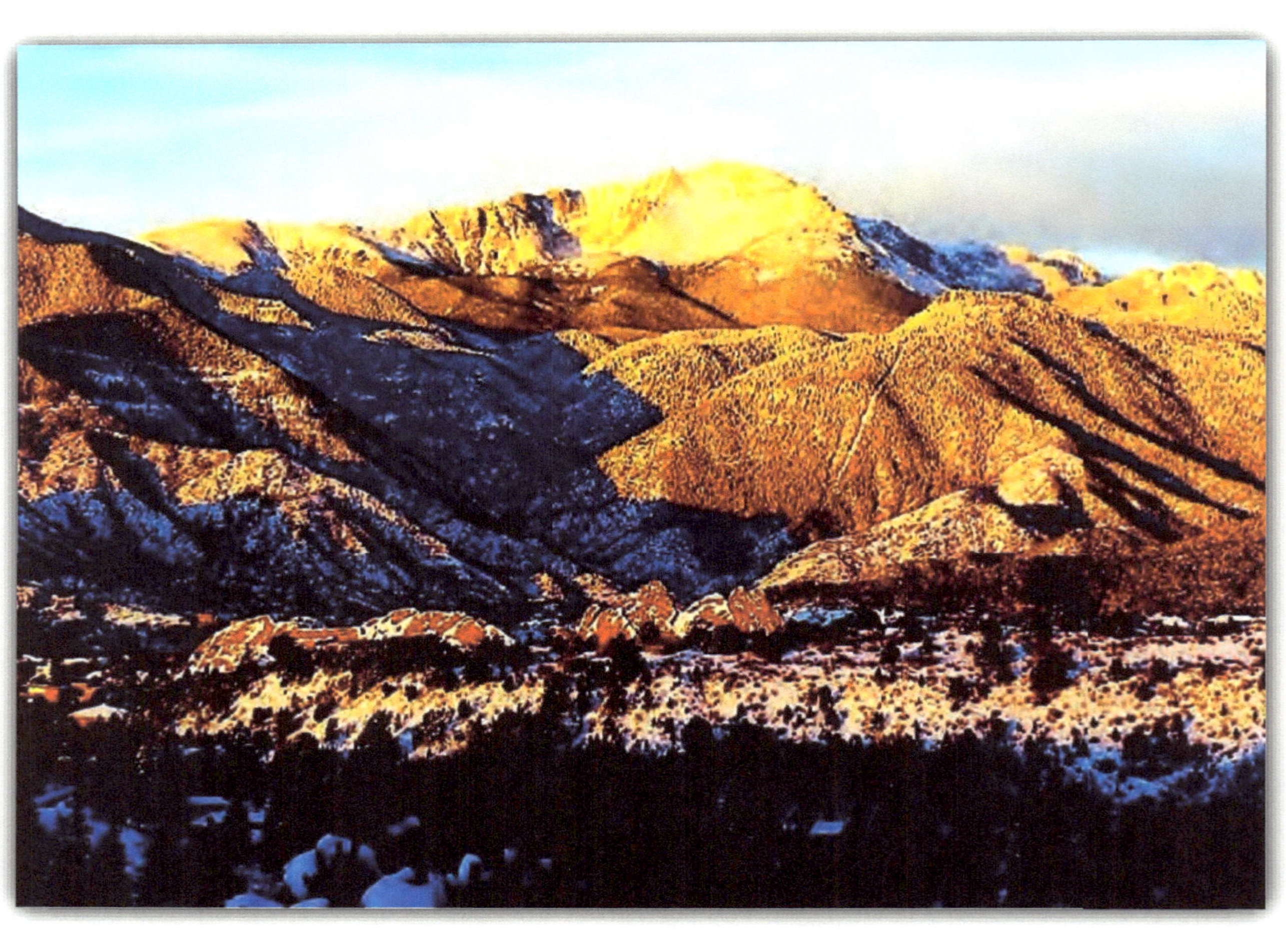

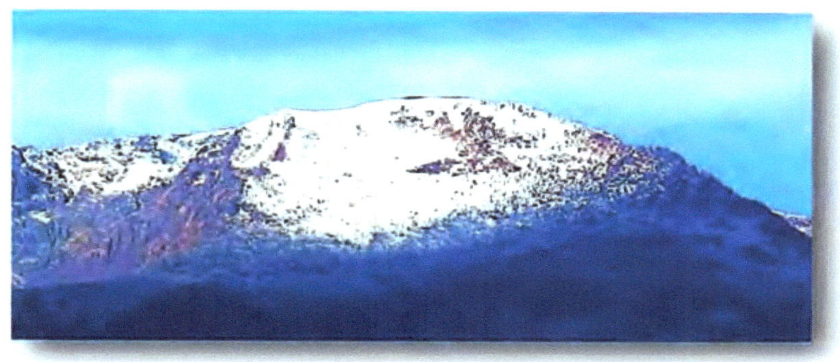

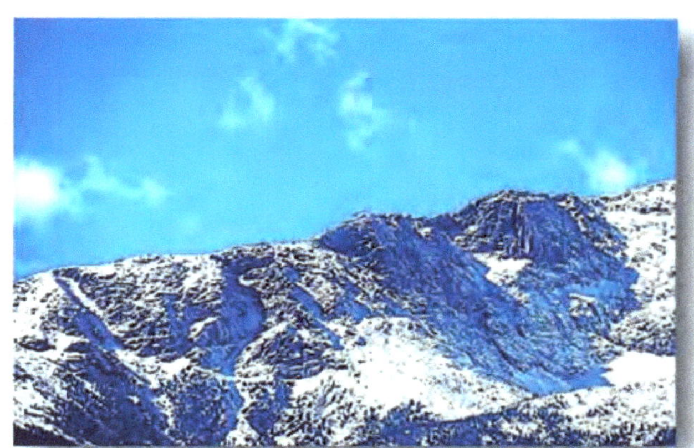

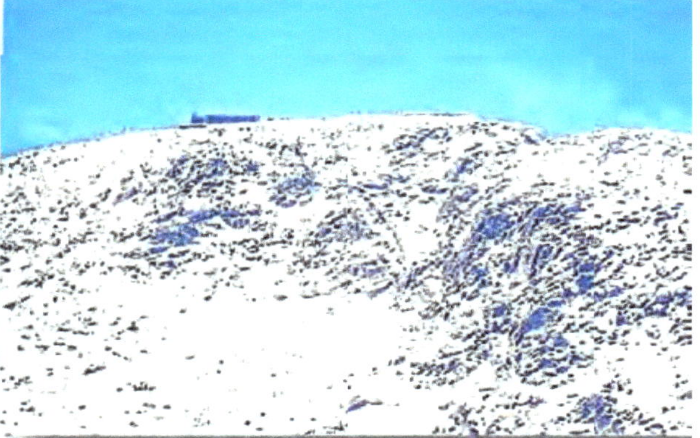

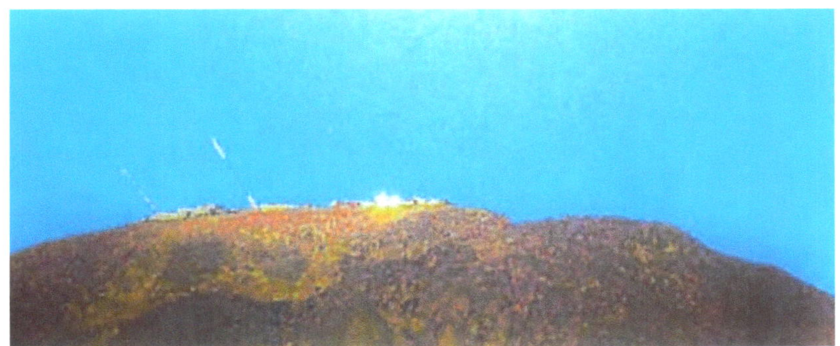

*When construction
of the new viewing center commenced in 2020,
two huge cranes appeared to bow in homage to the sun.*

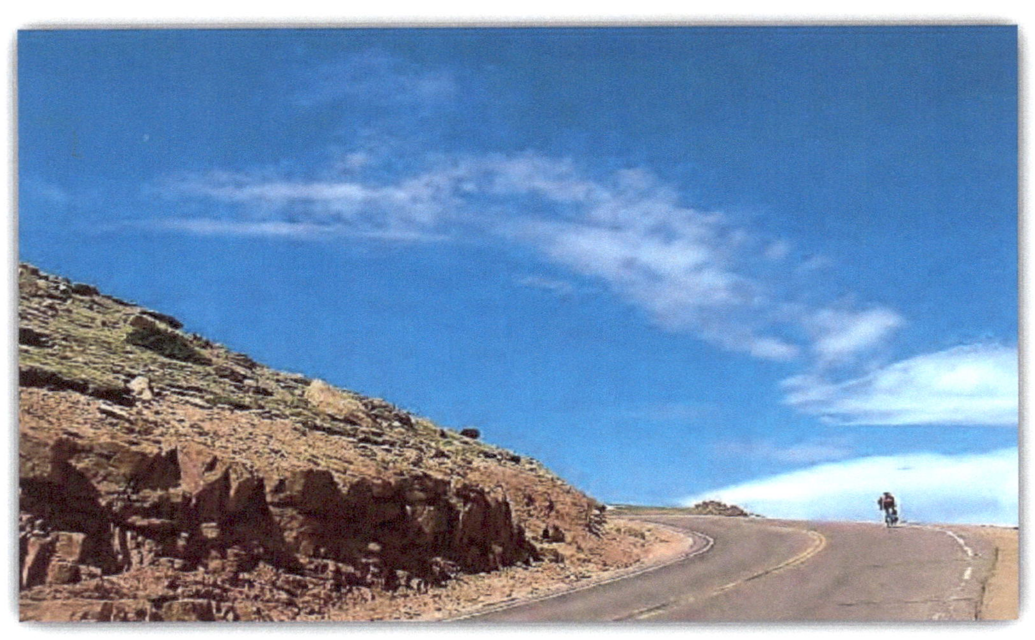

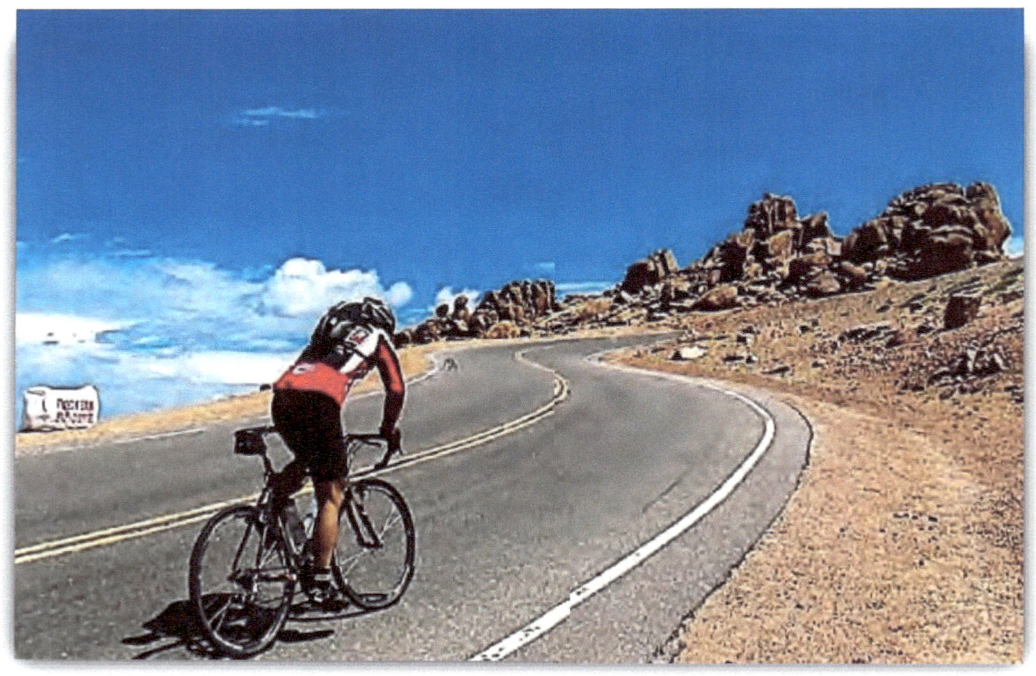

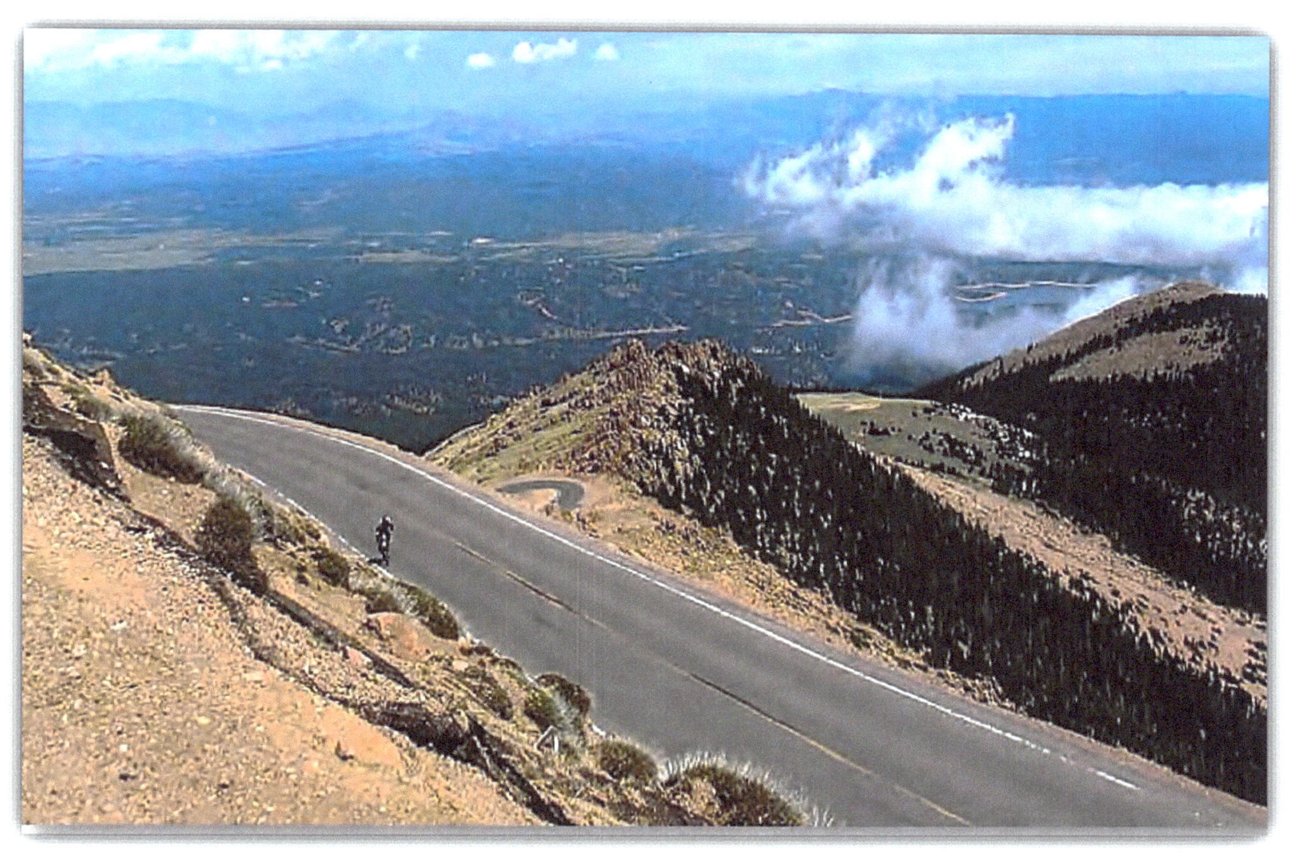

One June morning,
I decided to try driving to the top of Pikes Peak.
Half-way through the daunting climb,
I passed a bicyclist
peddling up the coiling pavement.
After exchanging a smile and a wave,
we leap-frogged all the way to the summit.

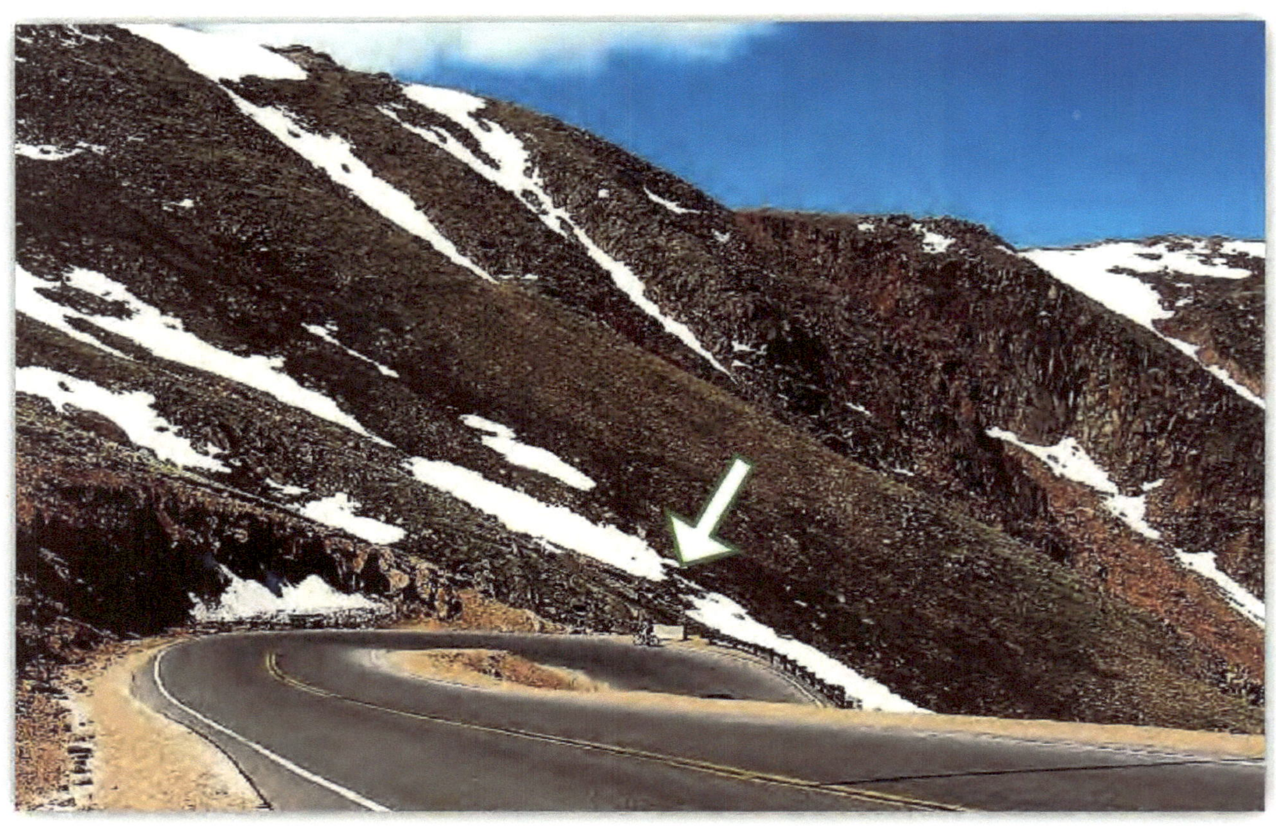

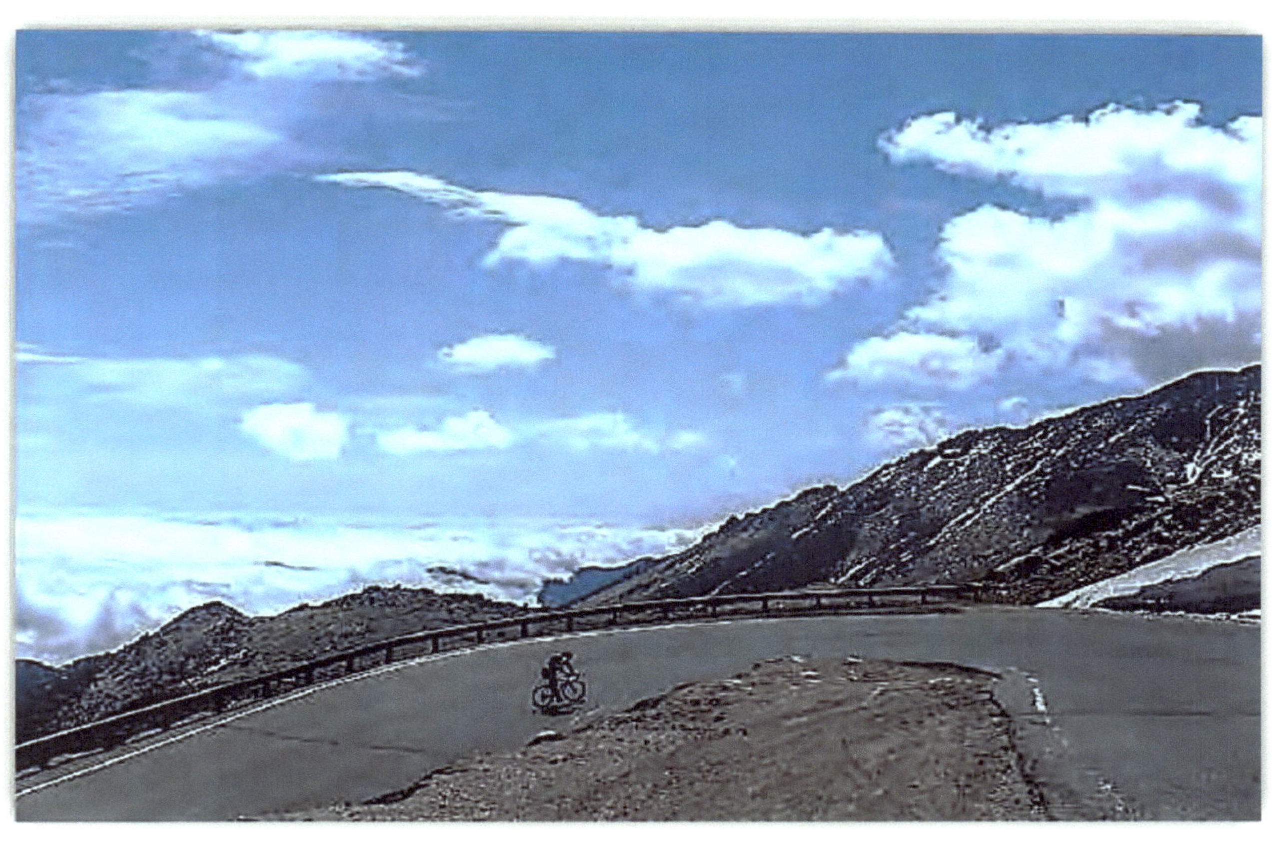

As we gained altitude,
the atmosphere started to grow gray.

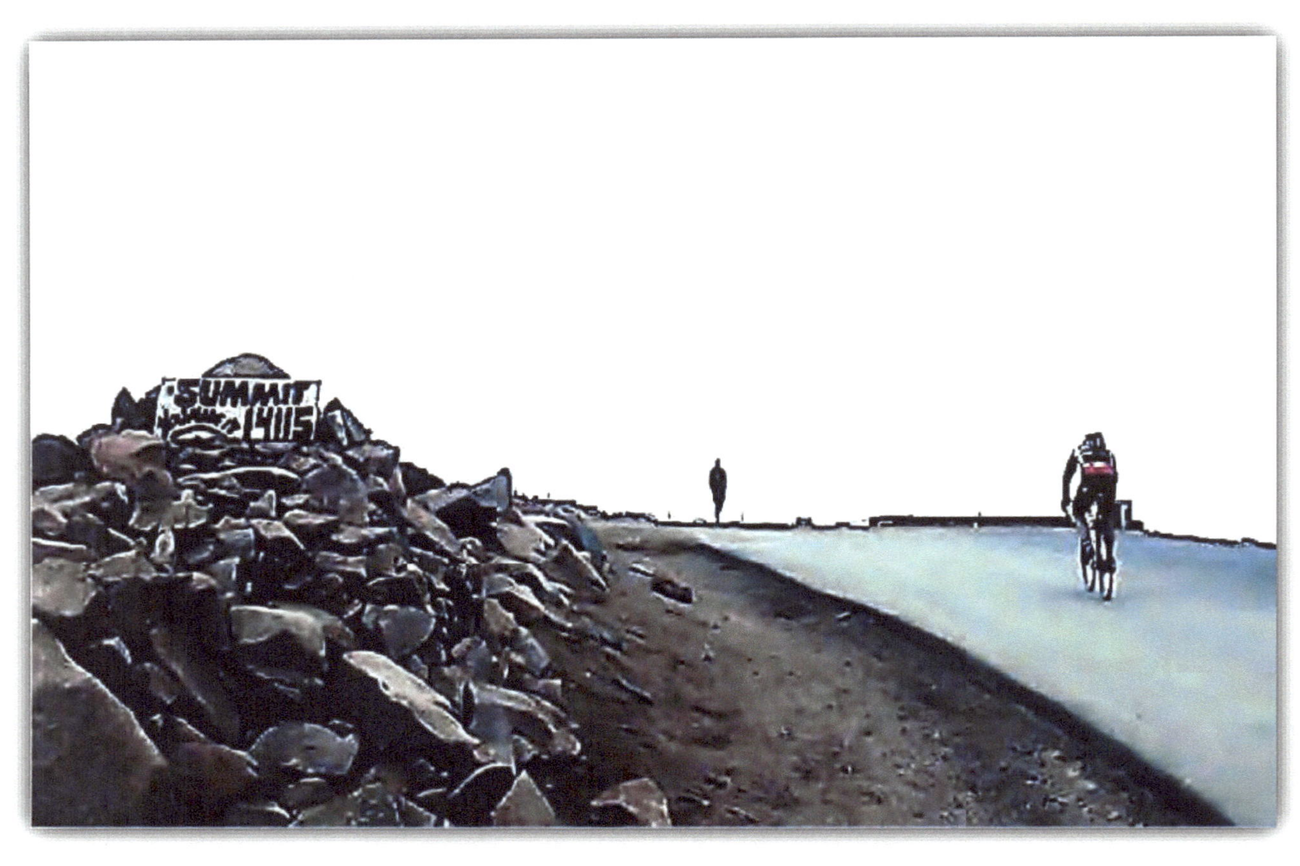

By the time we had reached the top,
we were shrouded in cloud.

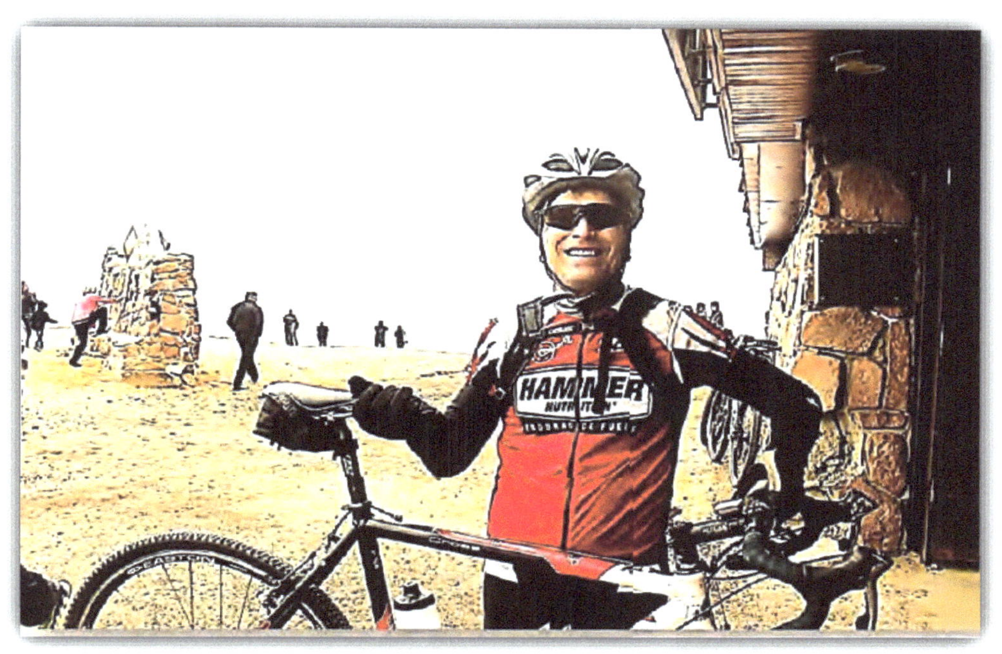

Ta-da!

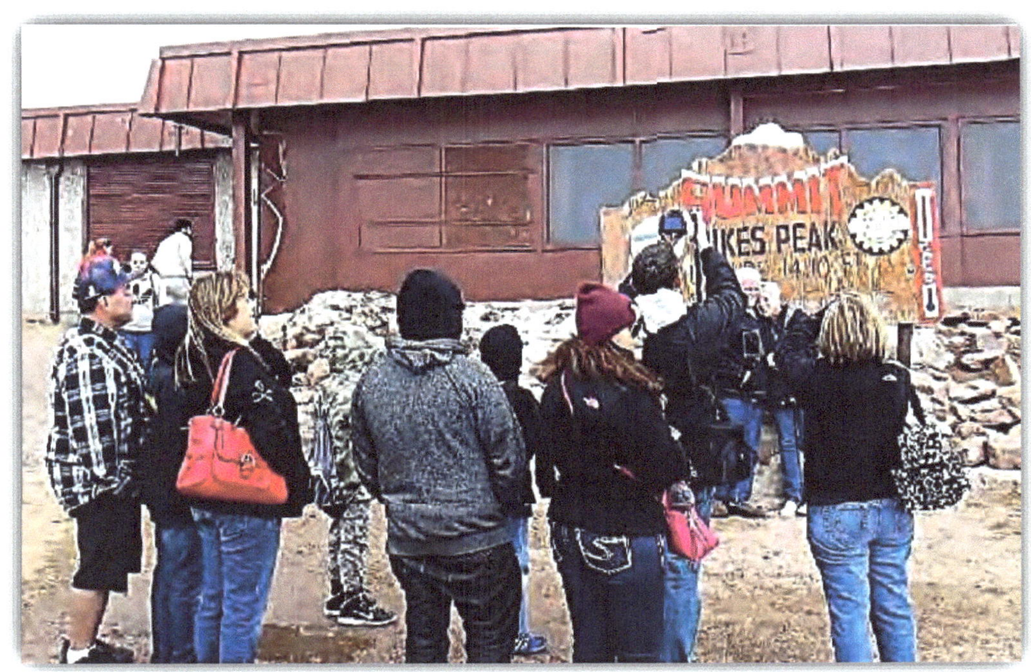

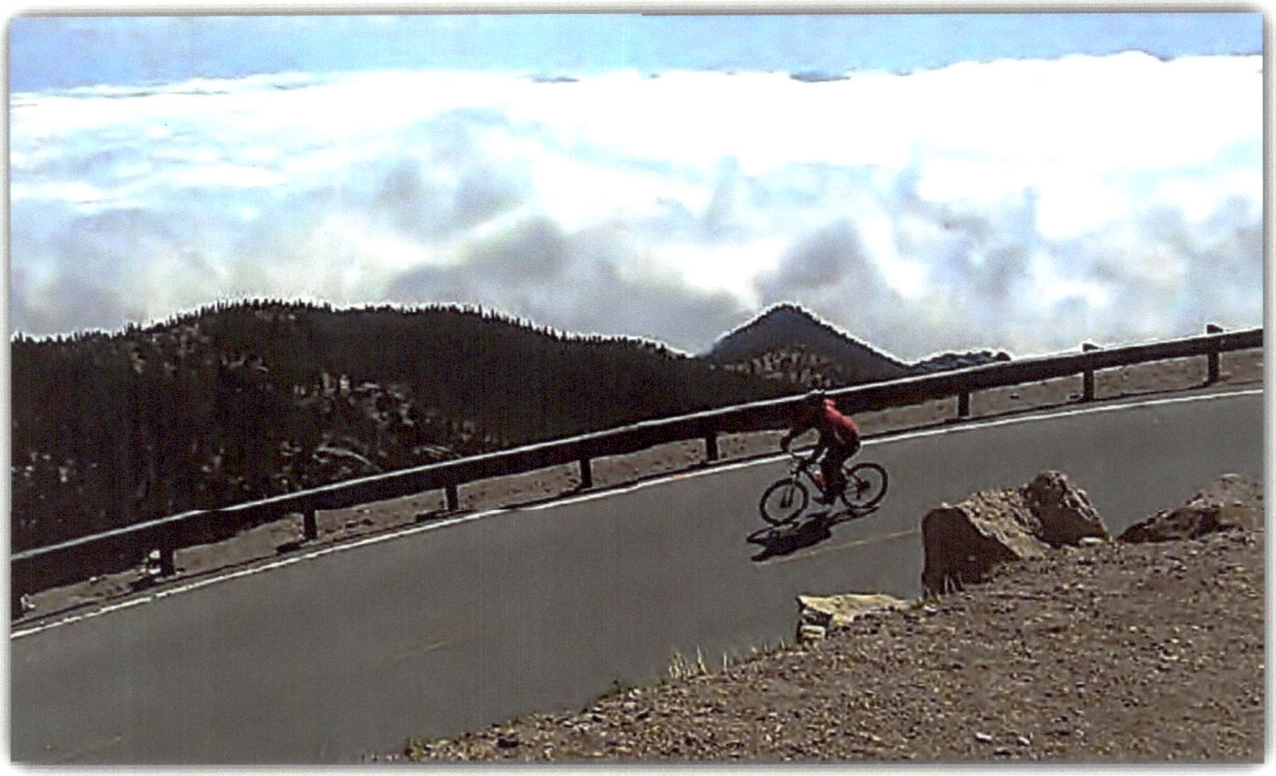

His quest complete, the wheeling warrior
hopped back onto his bike and headed homeward,
careening down the steep, undulating roadway.

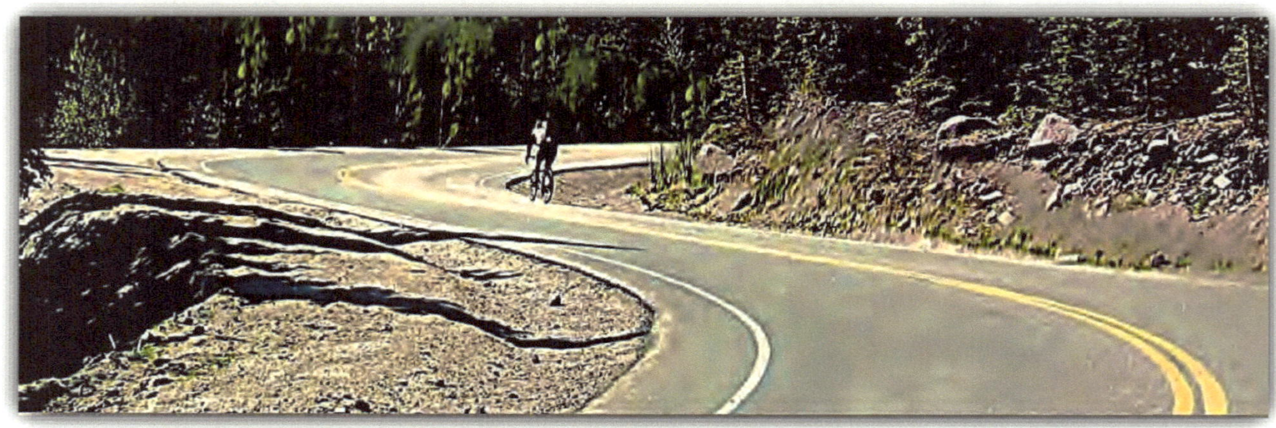

*So far, I had learned that
while some folks hiked, others biked,
and a few (like me) dared to drive.*

*But the most popular way to get
to the crown of "America's Mountain"
was to take the historic cog railroad,
owned and operated by the Broadmoor Hotel.
(Built during the gold rush era, its elegance
makes a stroll through this elegant five-star
Colorado Springs hotel a treat in itself.)*

*Departing from a quaint depot in Manitou Springs,
passengers hold onto their slanting bench seats,
while the little red train locks huge cogs onto
a center rail of gigantic sprockets, and slowly
-carefully-
crawls with its human cargo up to the visitors'
center (and a famous high-elevation donut shop)
at the summit.*

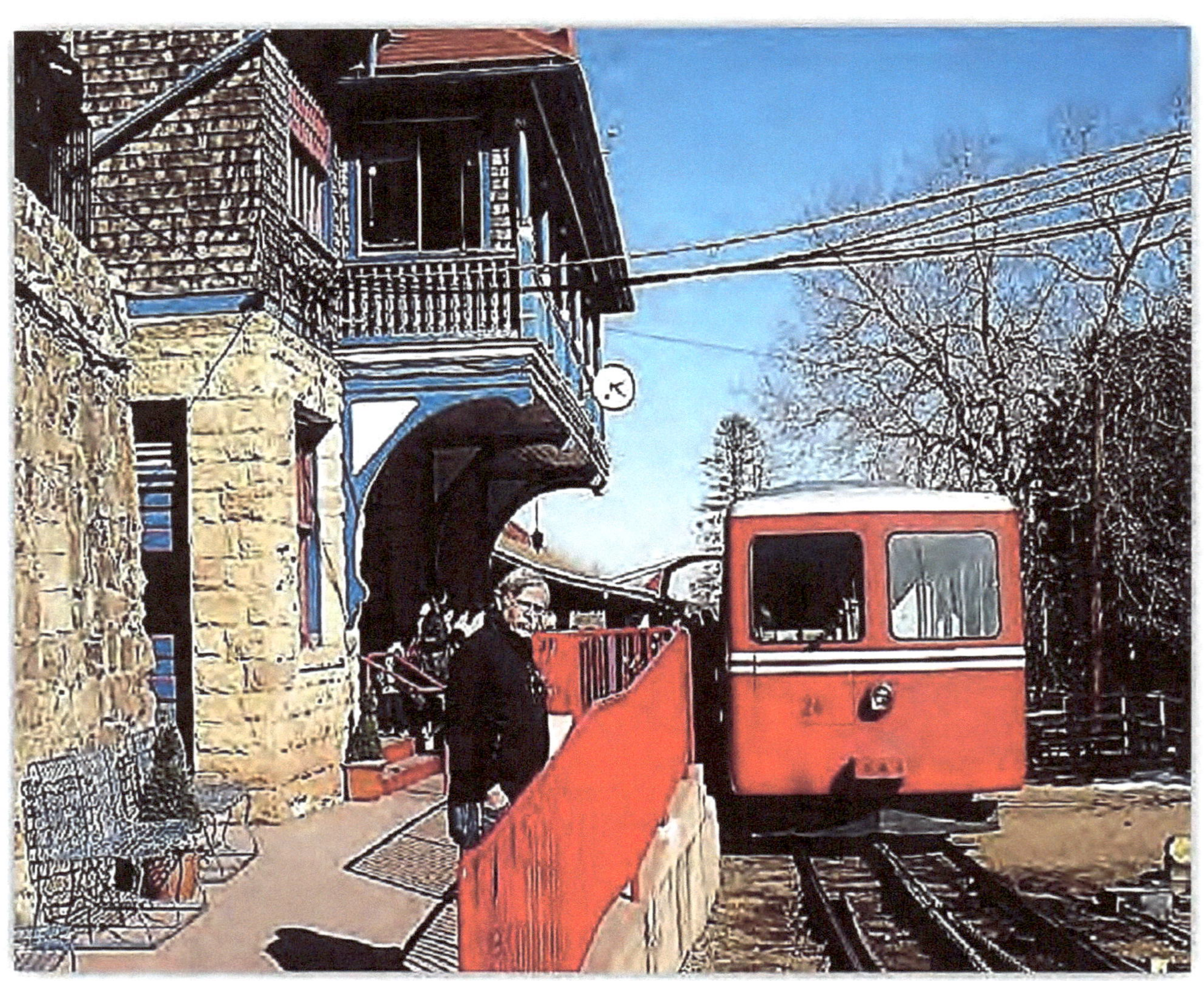

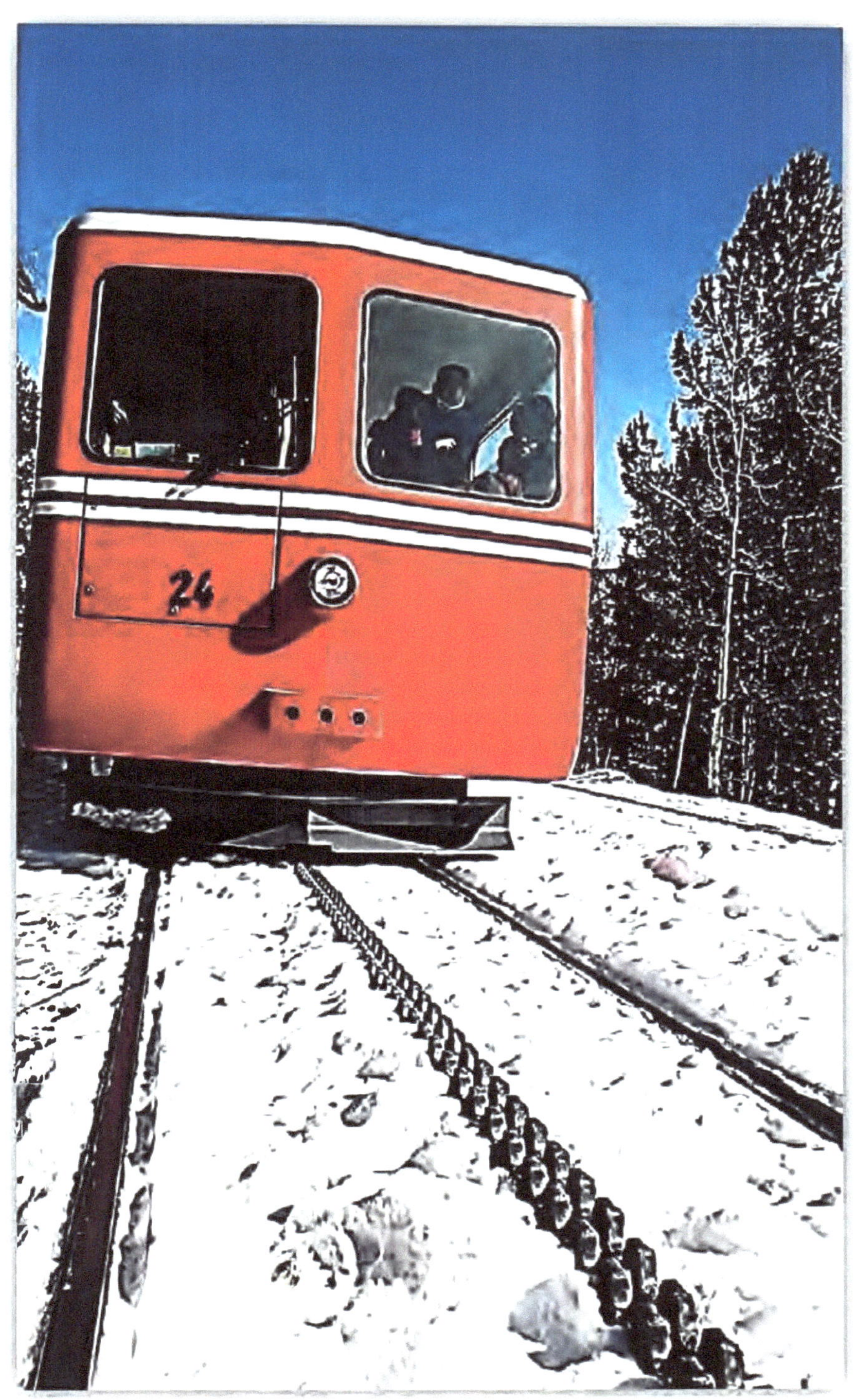

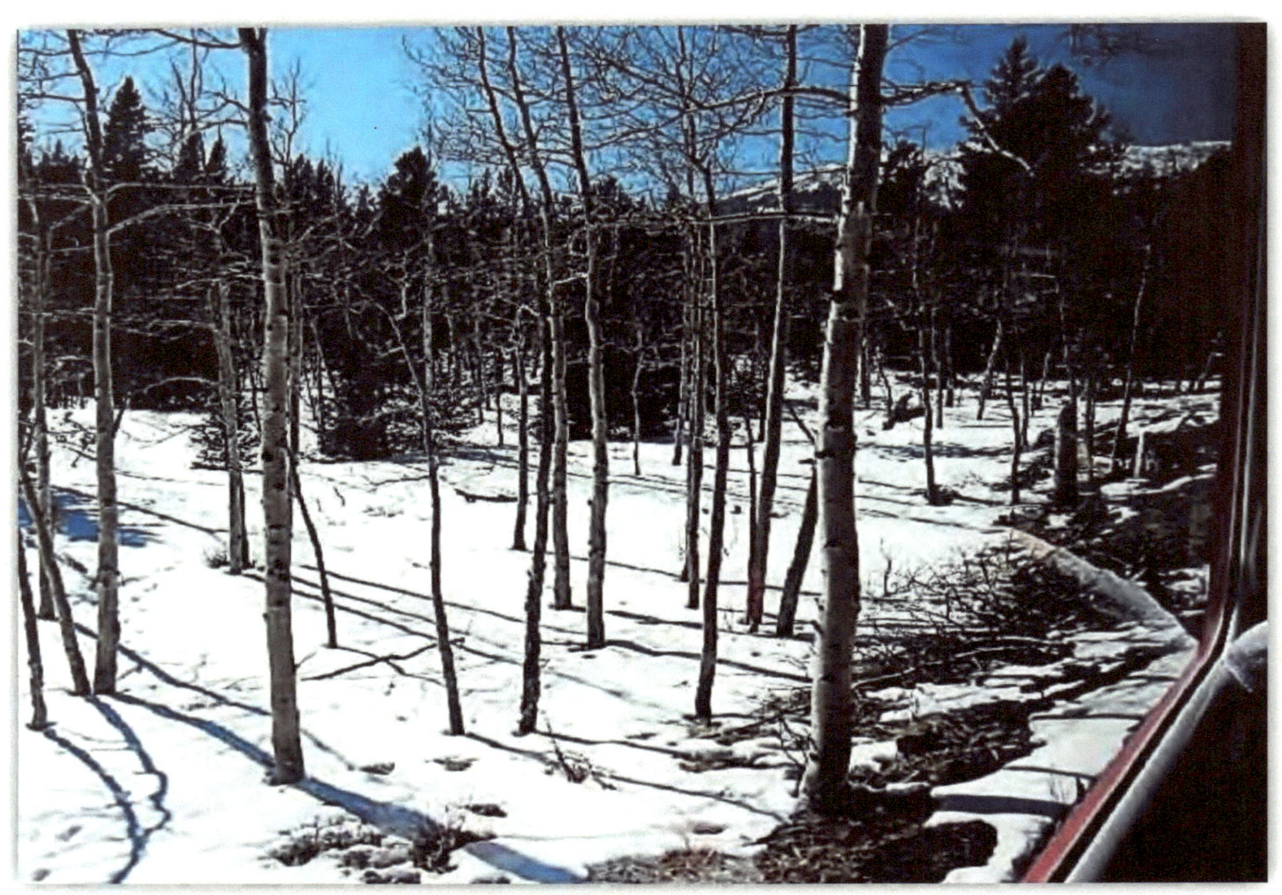

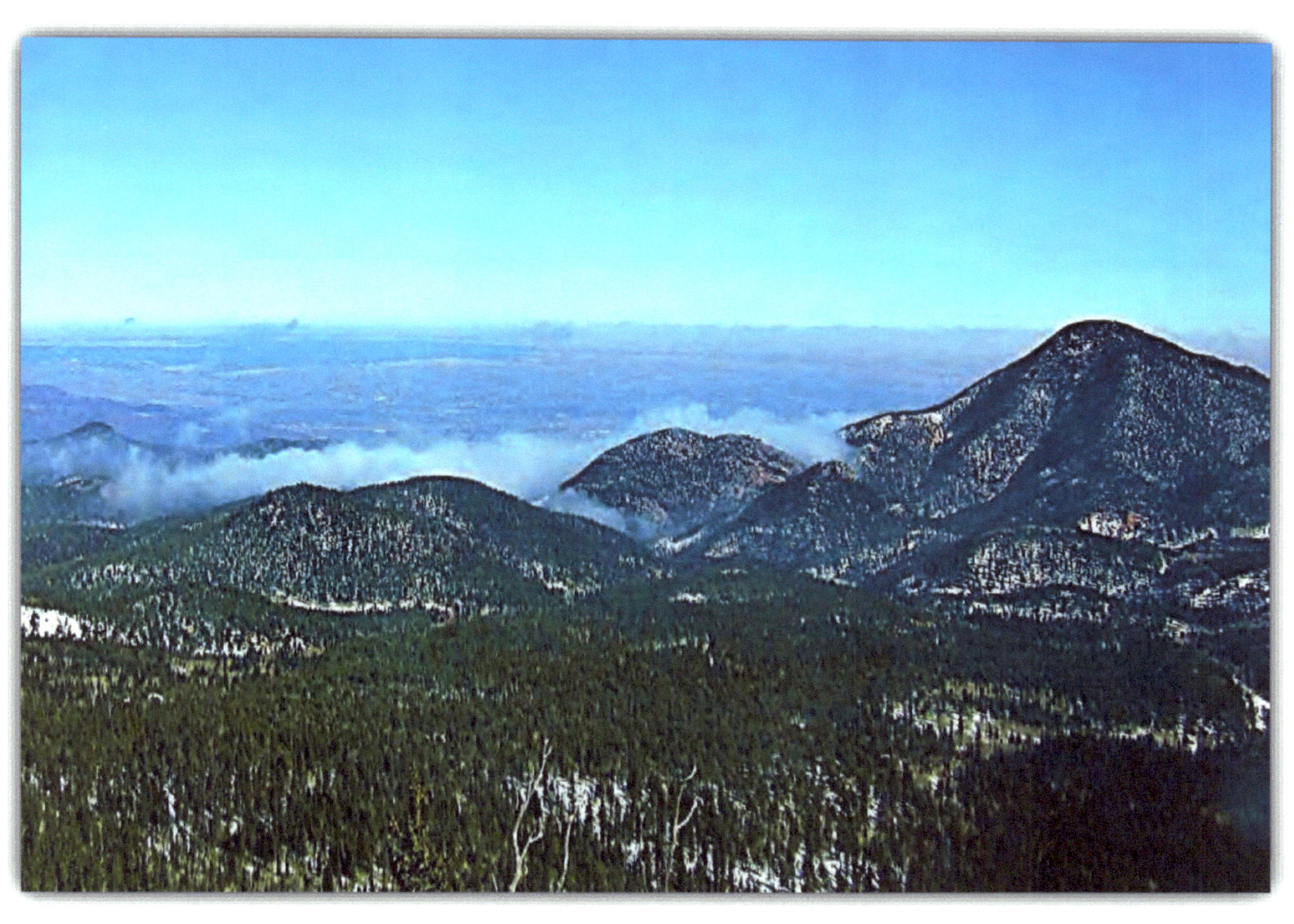

*When I rode on the train, I could imagine
that I was seeing all the way to Kansas.
And maybe I was!*

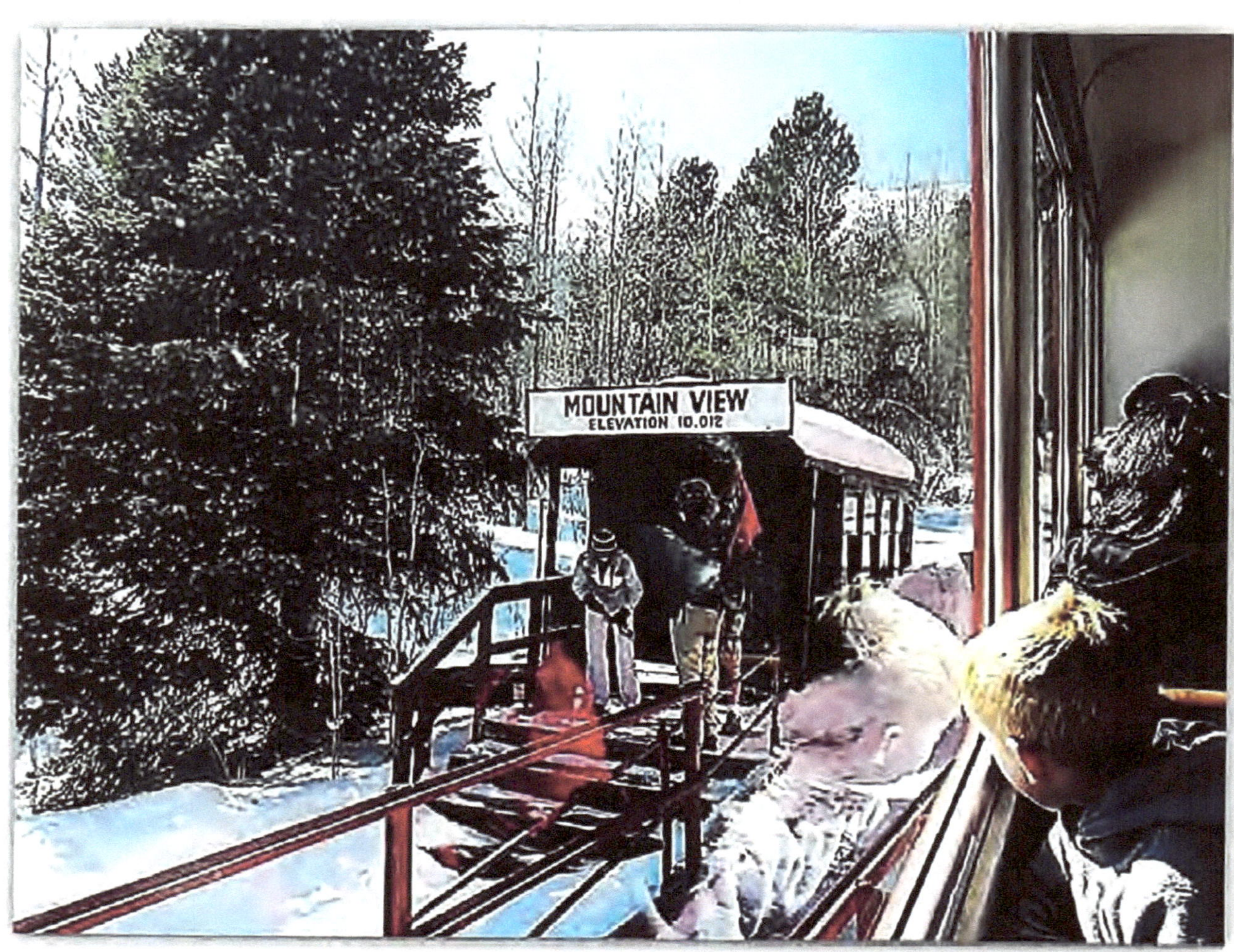

MOUNTAIN VIEW
ELEVATION 10.012

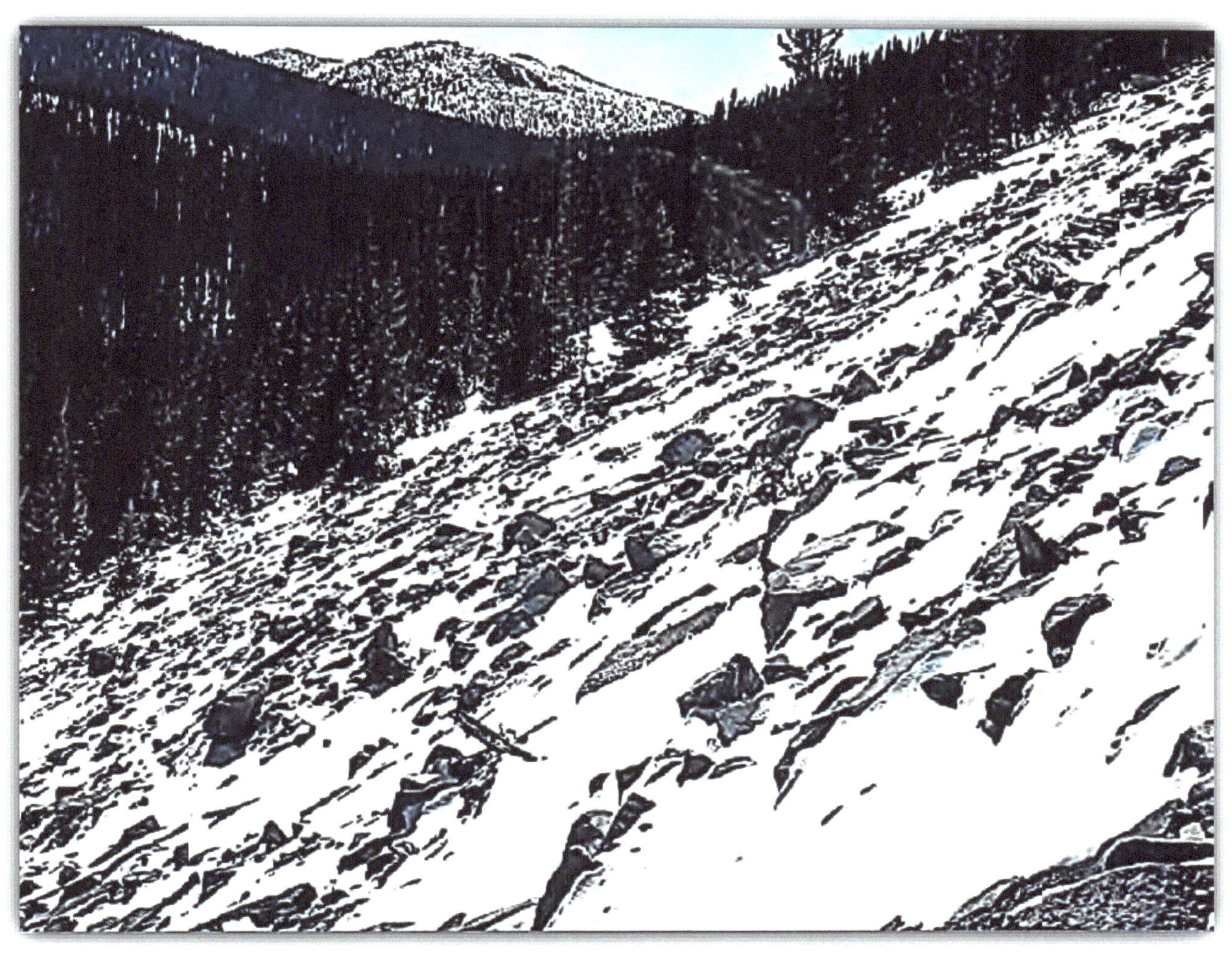

*I found stopping in a field of scree under full sun
to be sort of fun.*

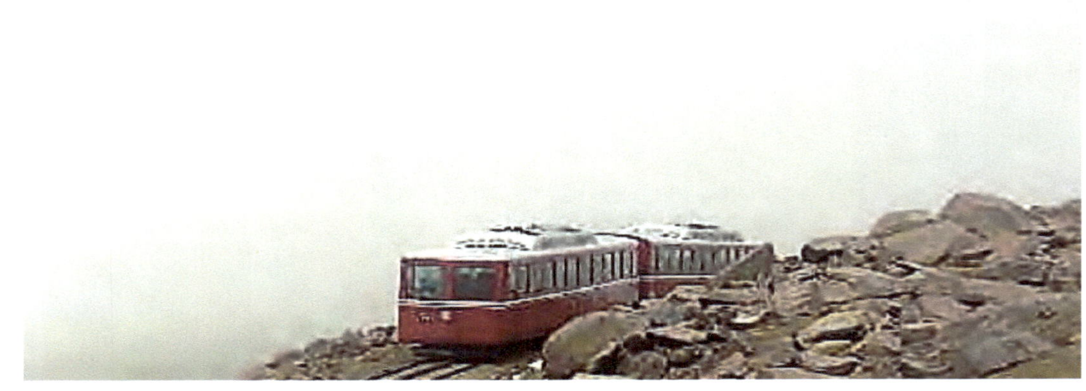

But the weather higher-up does not always cooperate.

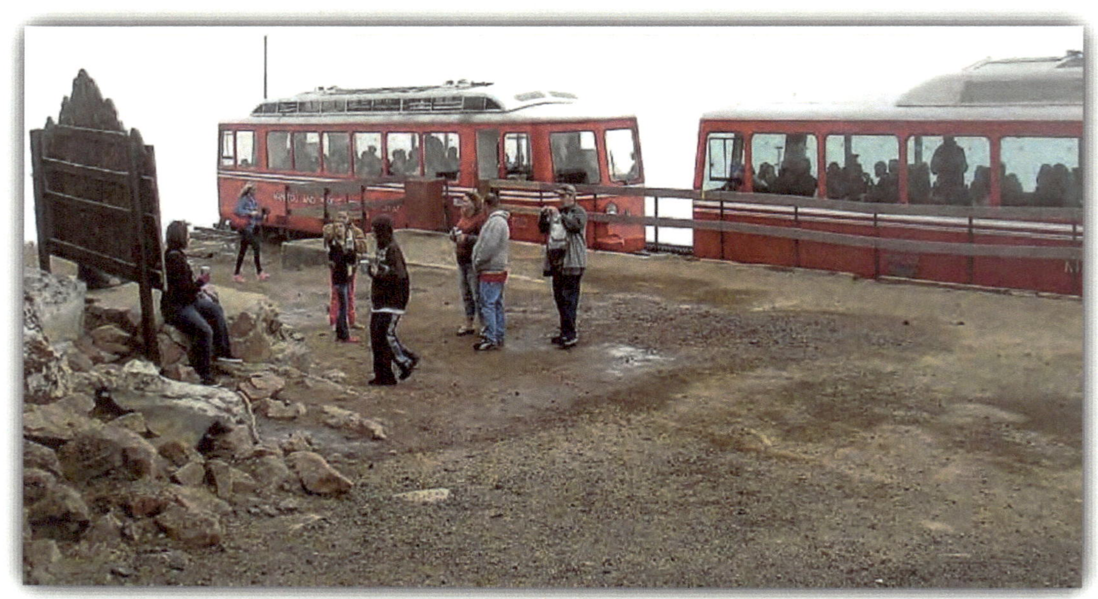

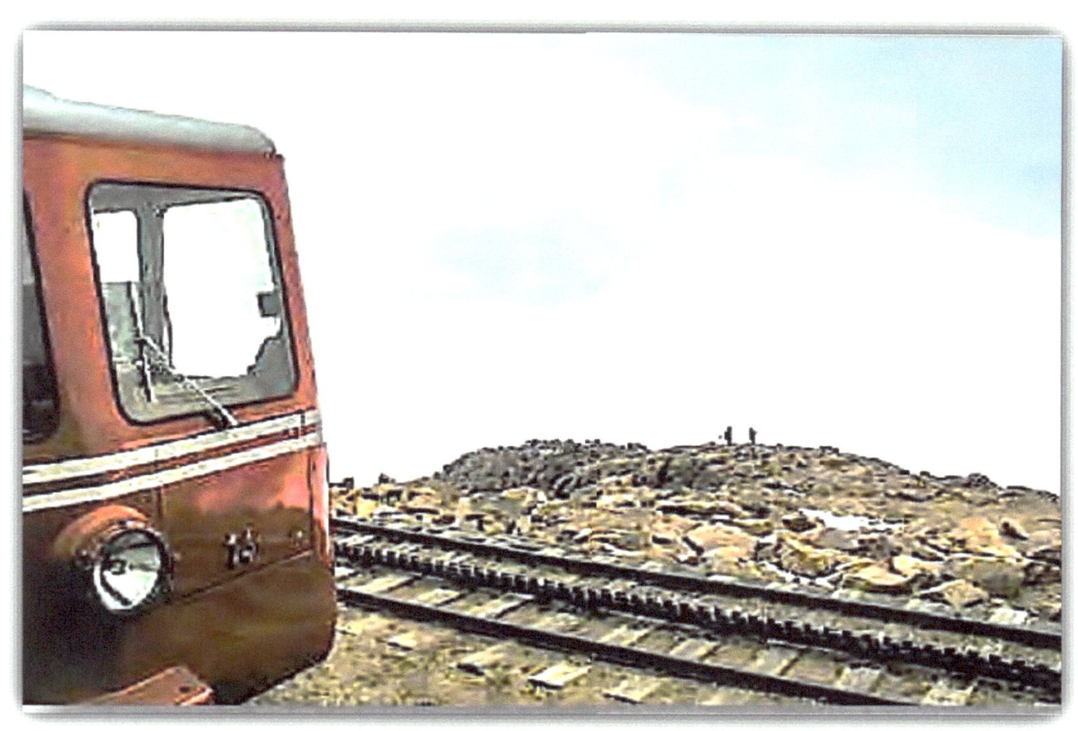

"*All aboard!*"

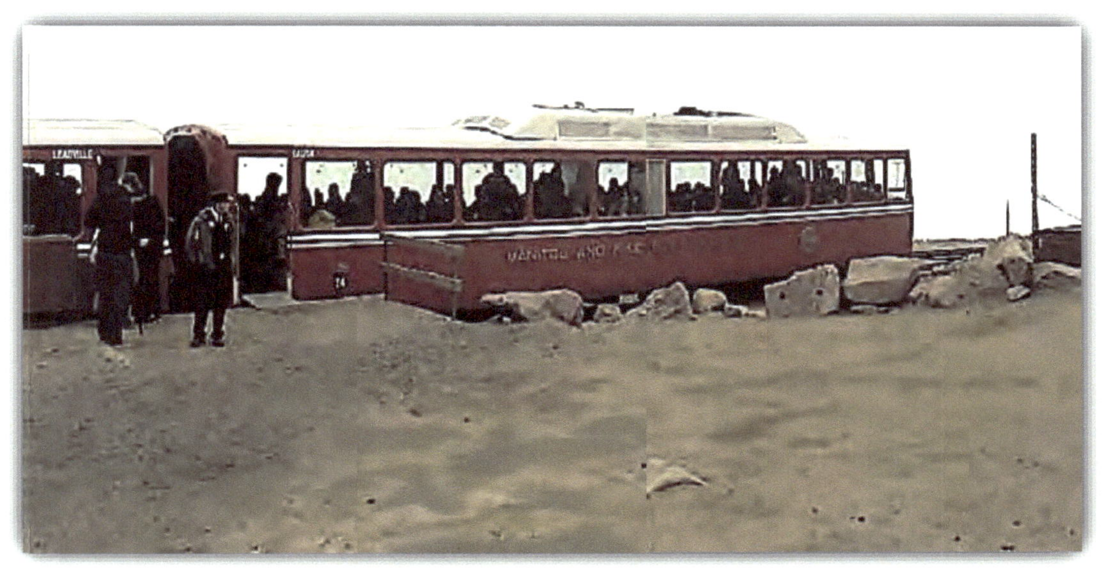

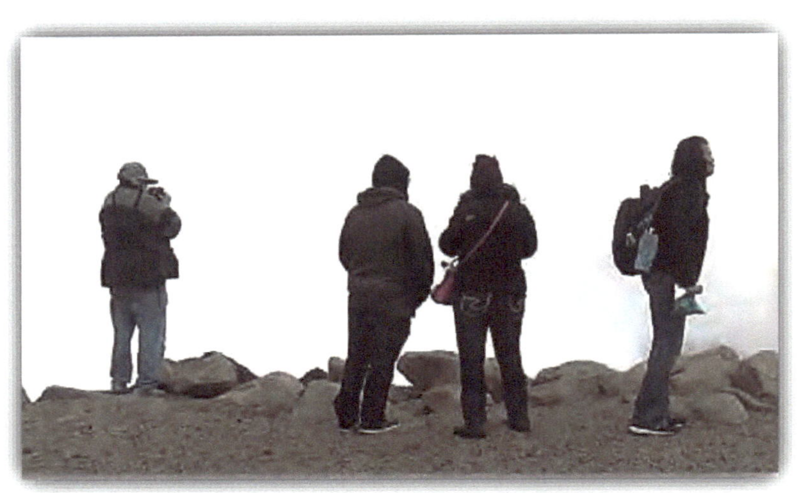

When fog engulfs the showcase view at the top,
visitors might have only an *enigmatic* description
of standing at the edge of the world
−gazing into nothingness−
to share with friends back home.

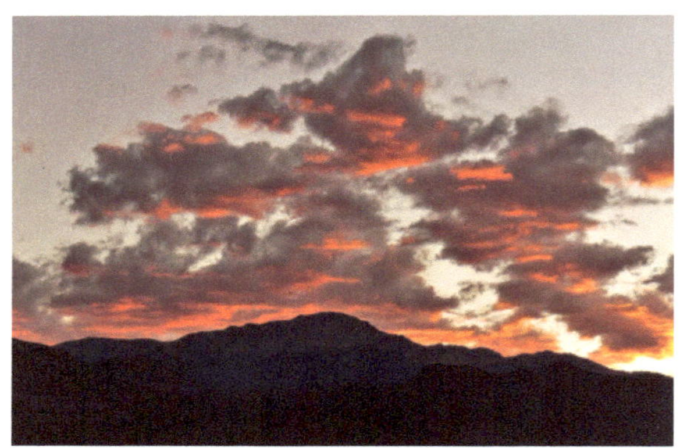

Sometimes,
a mountain really <u>is</u>
". . . best, when seen from the plain!"

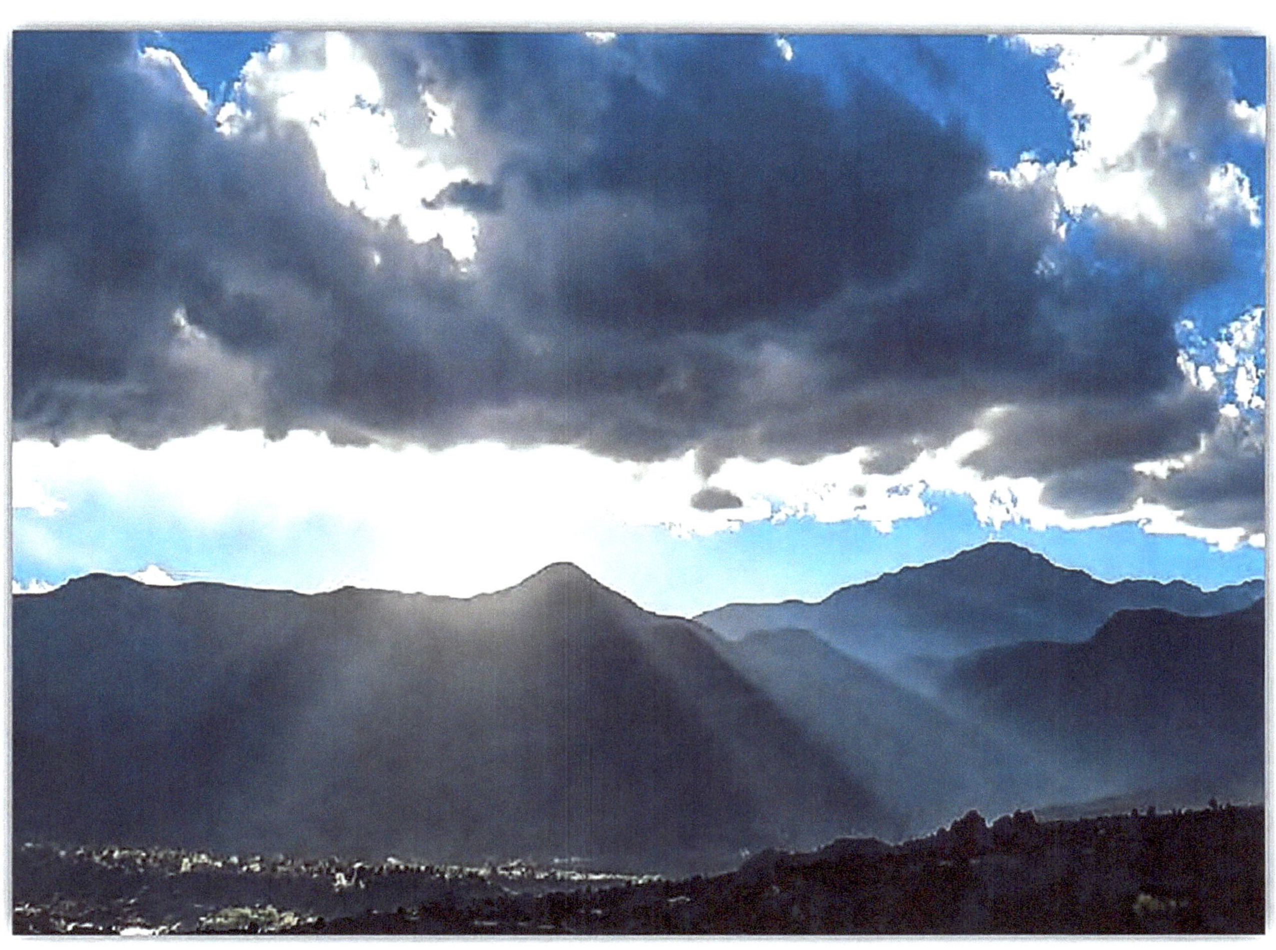

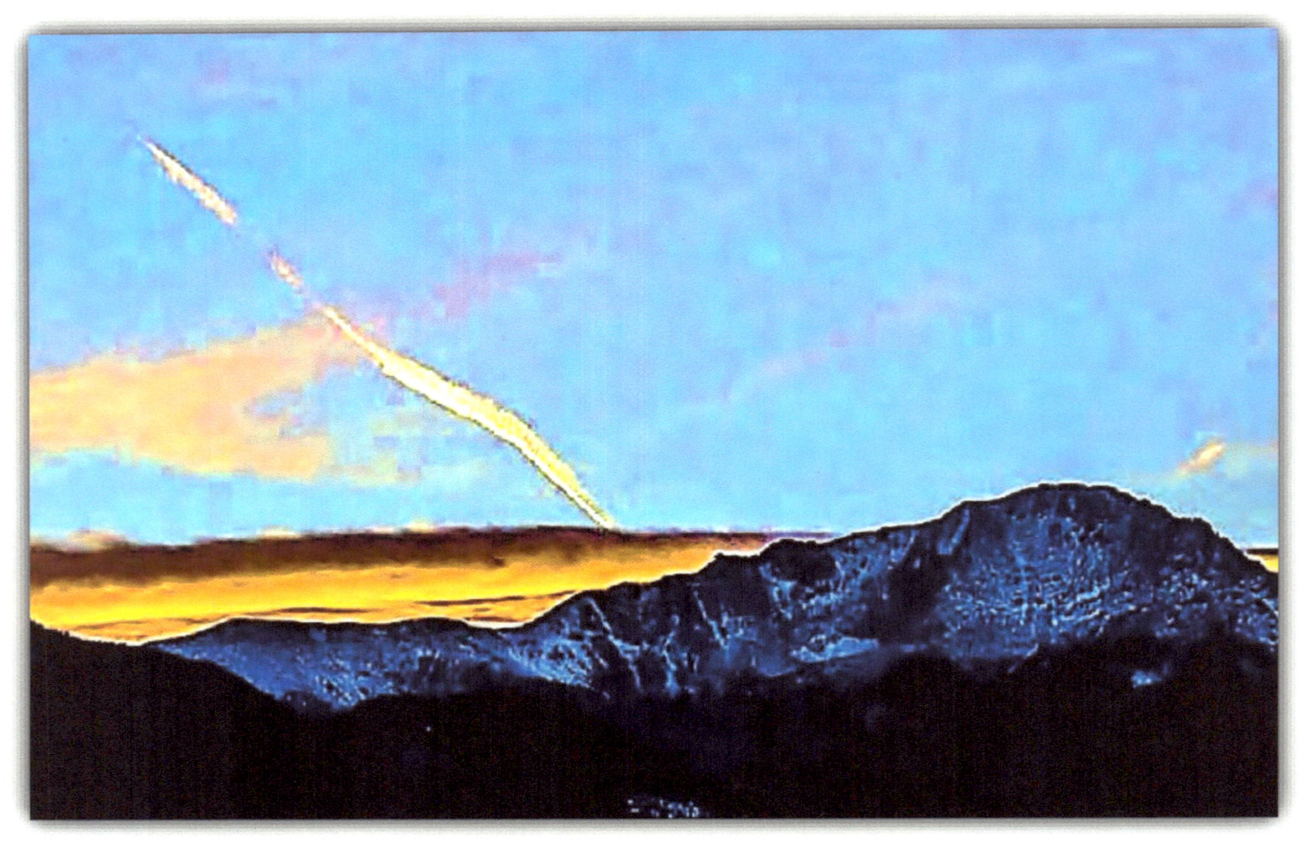

*Watching from our deck, we were rewarded on many
an evening as the sun sank behind the horizon,
sending up long fiery rays into the clouds
and drenching them with fantastic washes of color.*

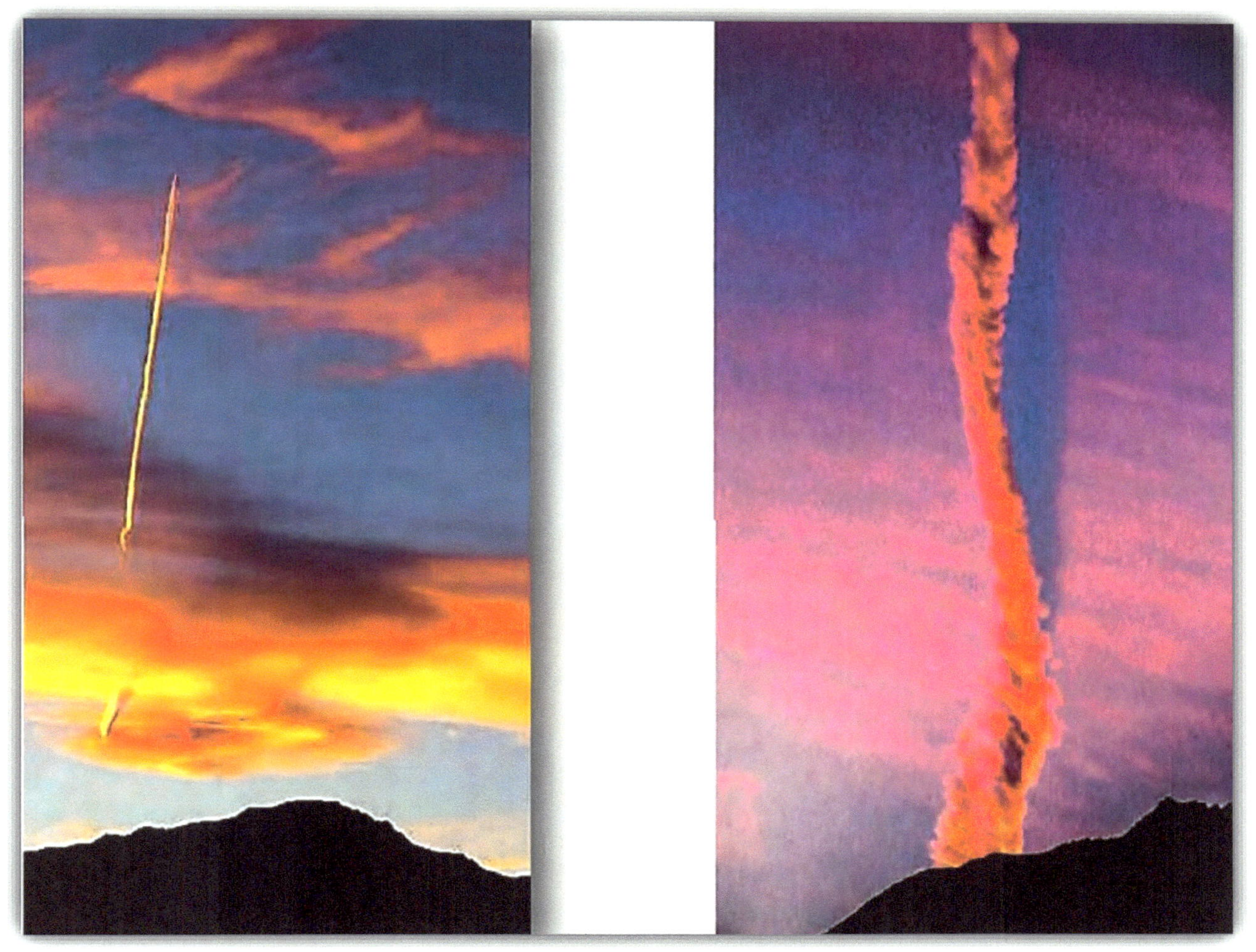

Almost daily,
jets carrying passengers to and from the West
left behind fascinating contrails that pierced
through the clouds or waffled with the wind.

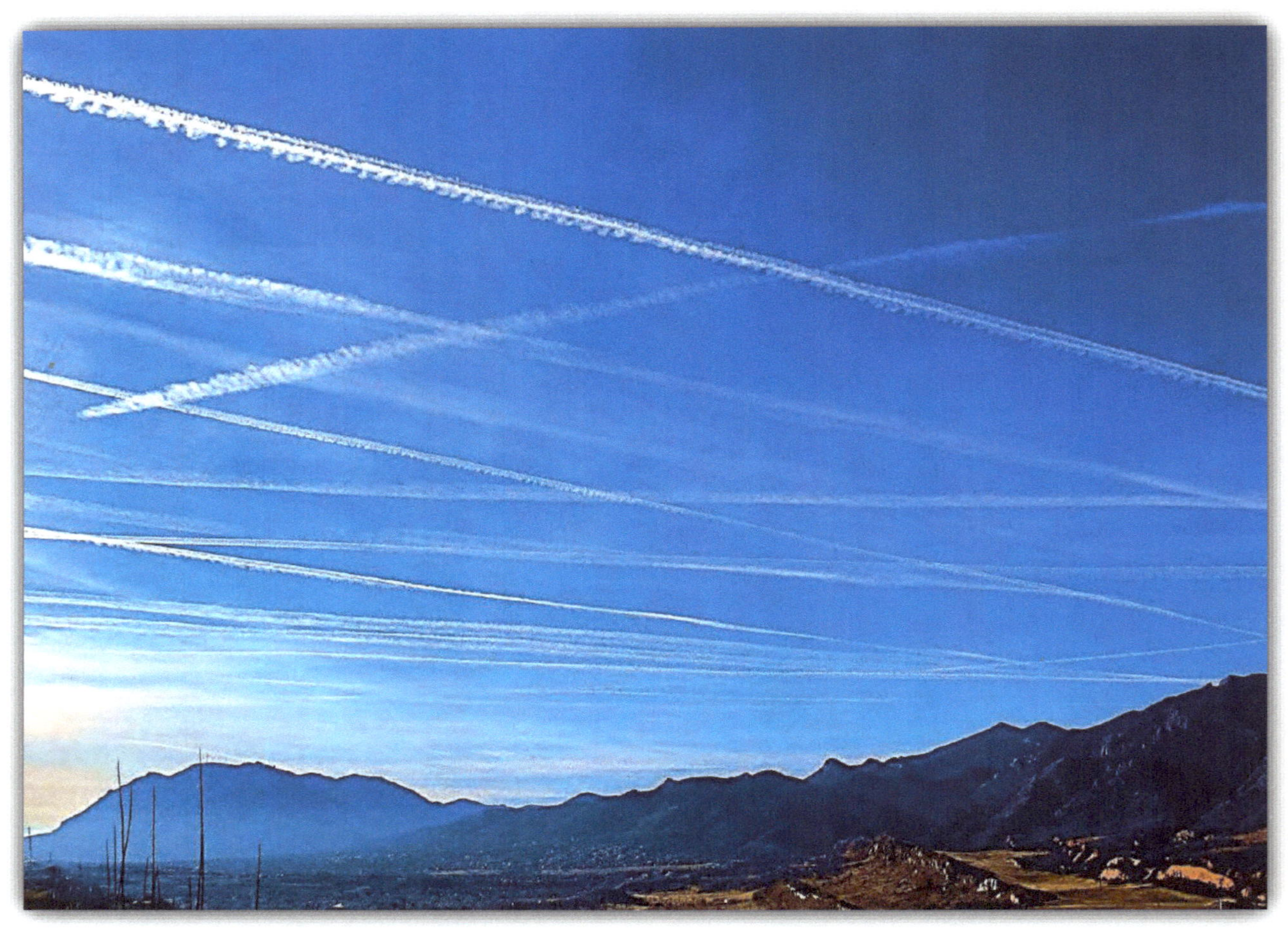

*When afternoon conditions were just right,
multiple lines might linger overhead,
cross—hatching the sky and pointing at the
sequestered home of NORAD, which
hunkers beneath a mantle of solid granite.*

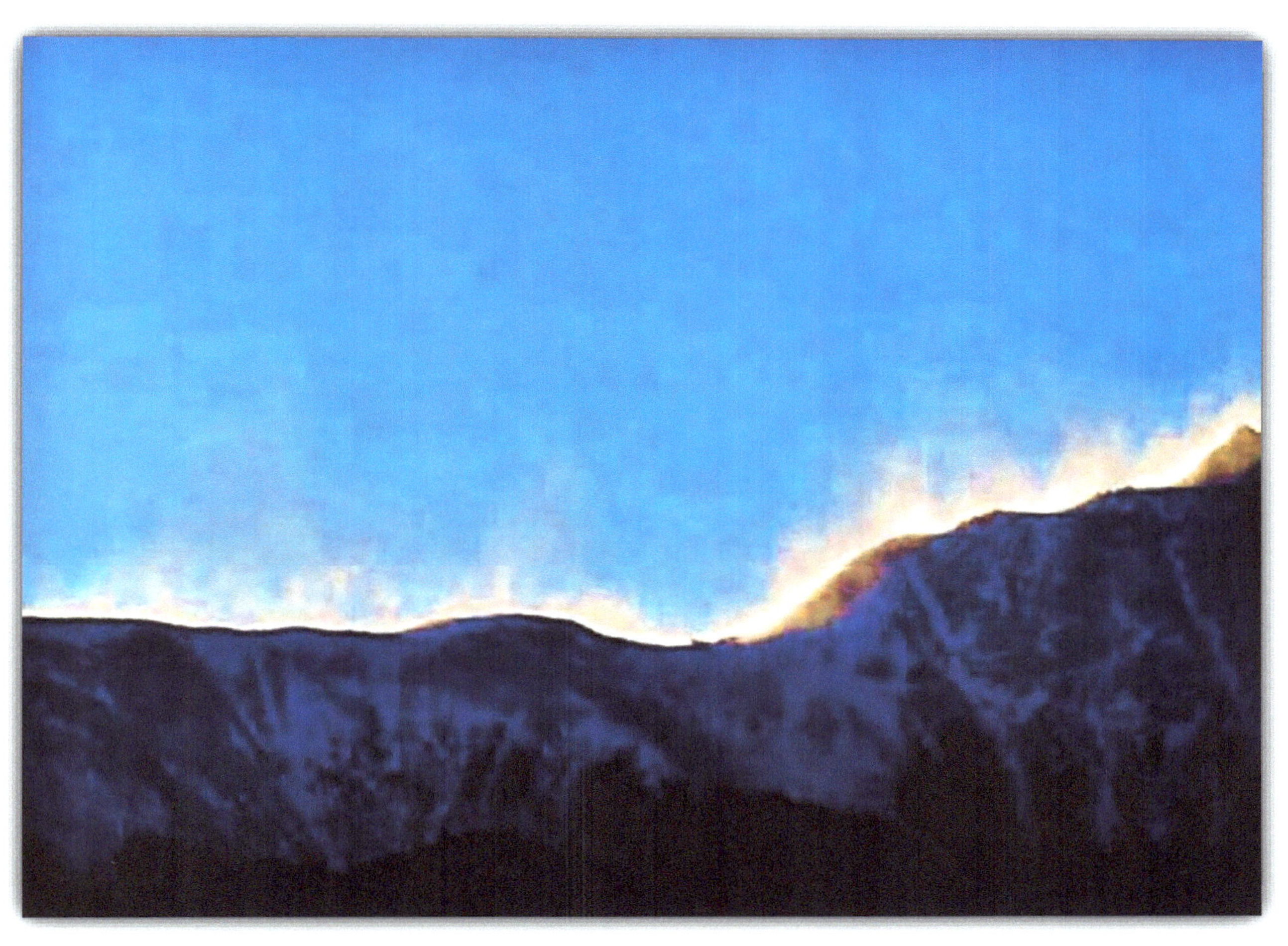

In strong winds,
blustering snow looked like
a galloping horse's mane.

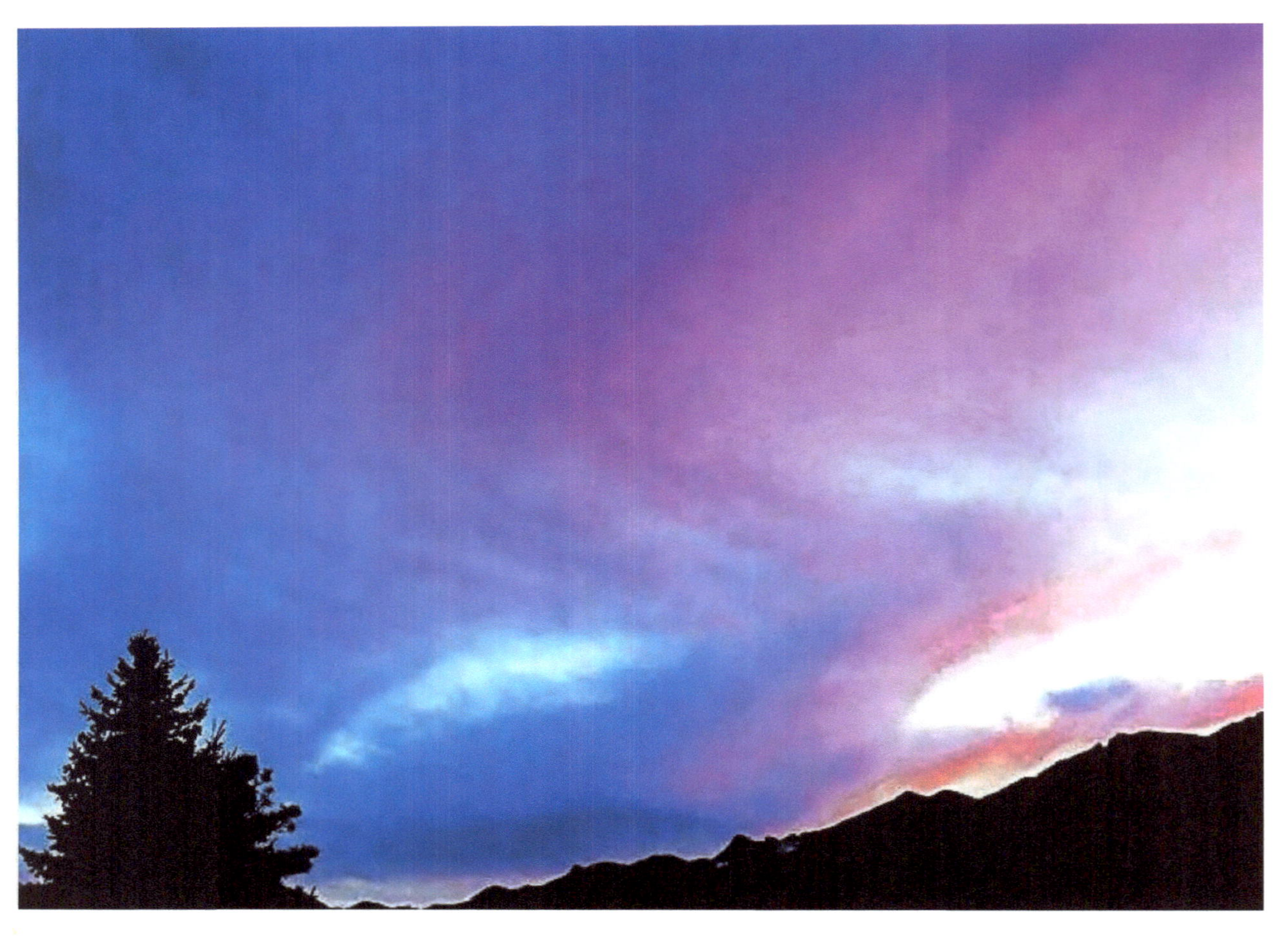

It amused me whenever
the wind changed its mind
and zig-zagged back on itself.

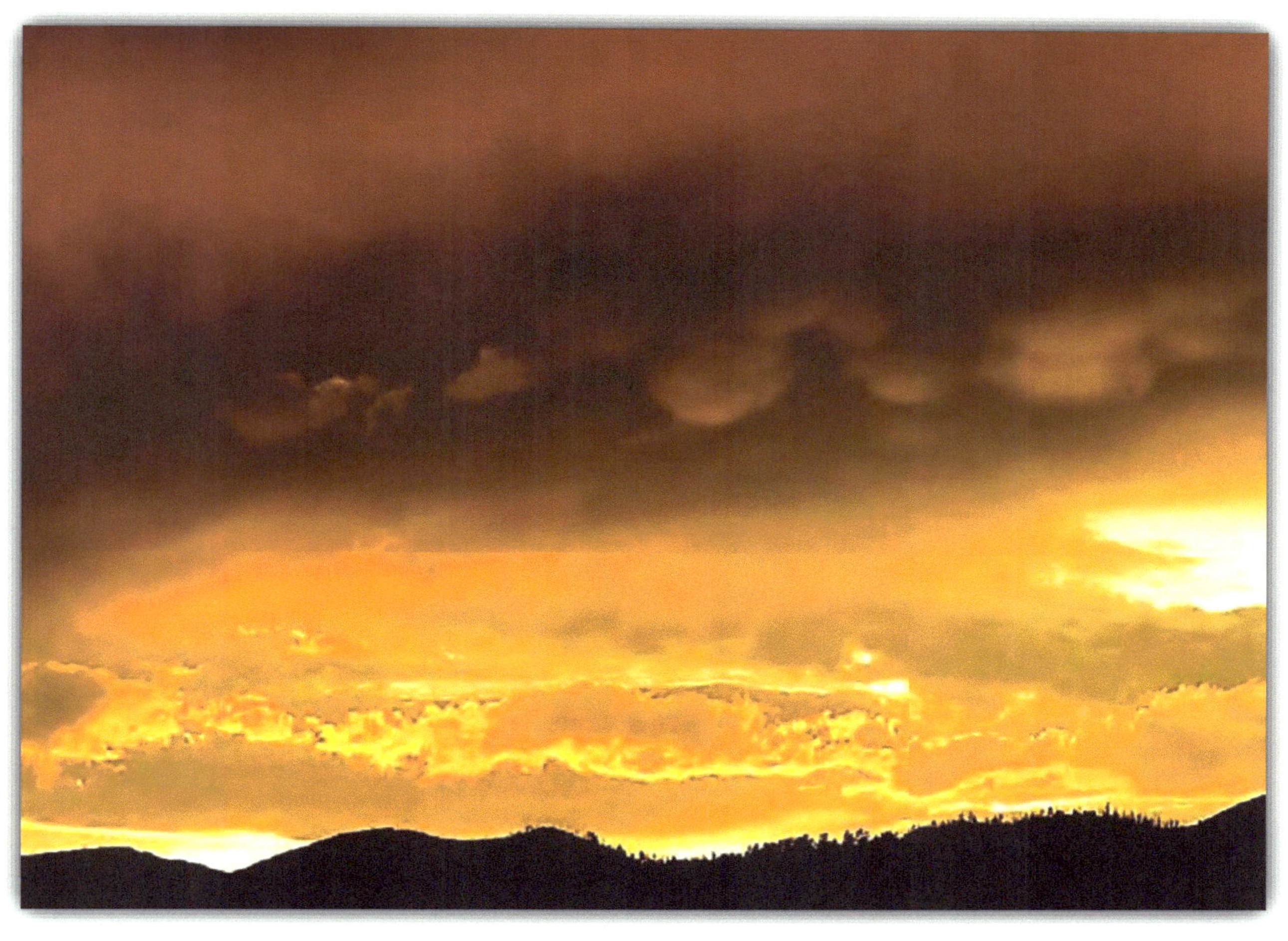

I especially liked the soft-looking baby bums that bumped by above the ridge.

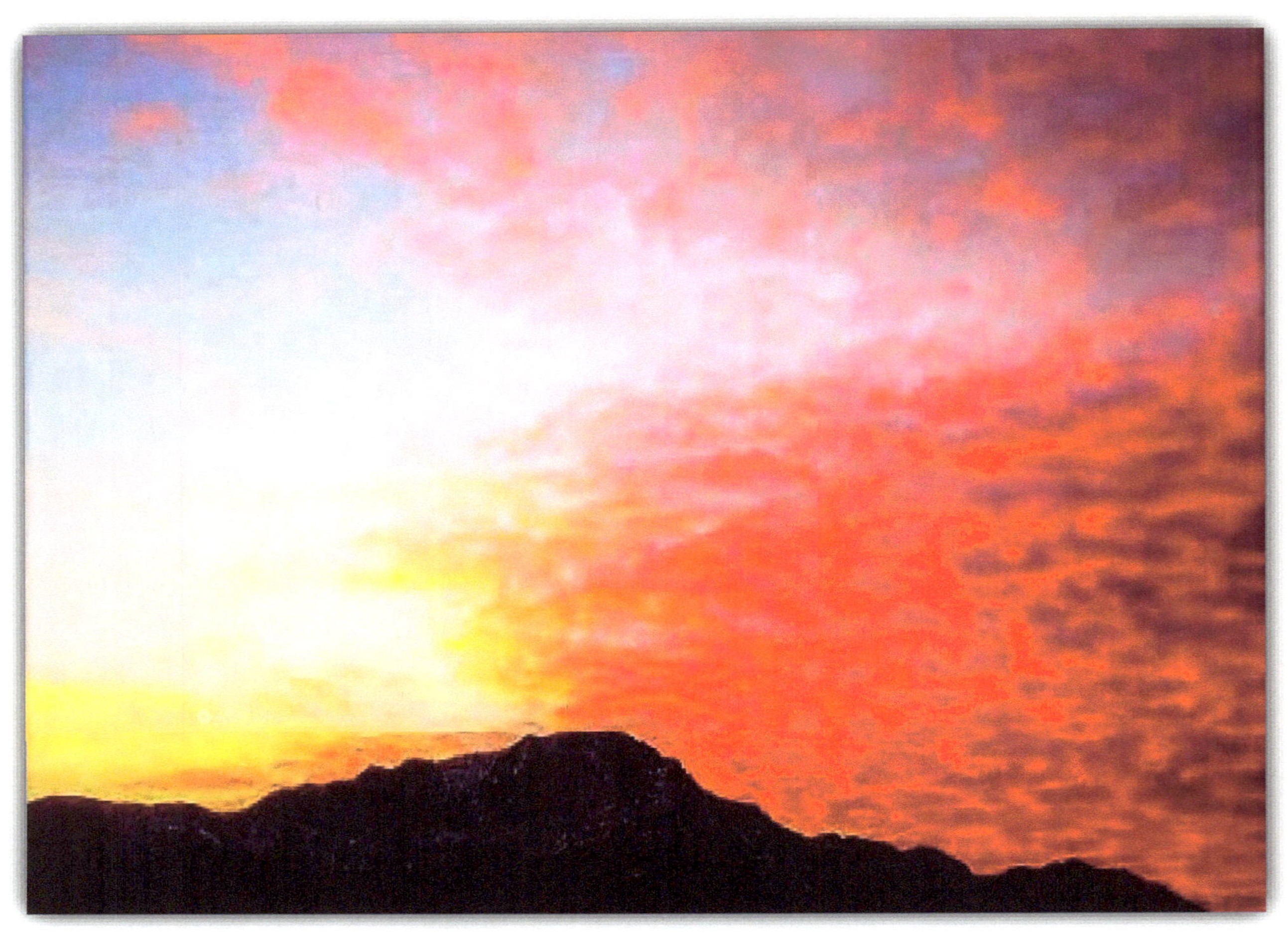

*Once, the mountain created such dramatic drag
that it seemed to tear the sky in two.*

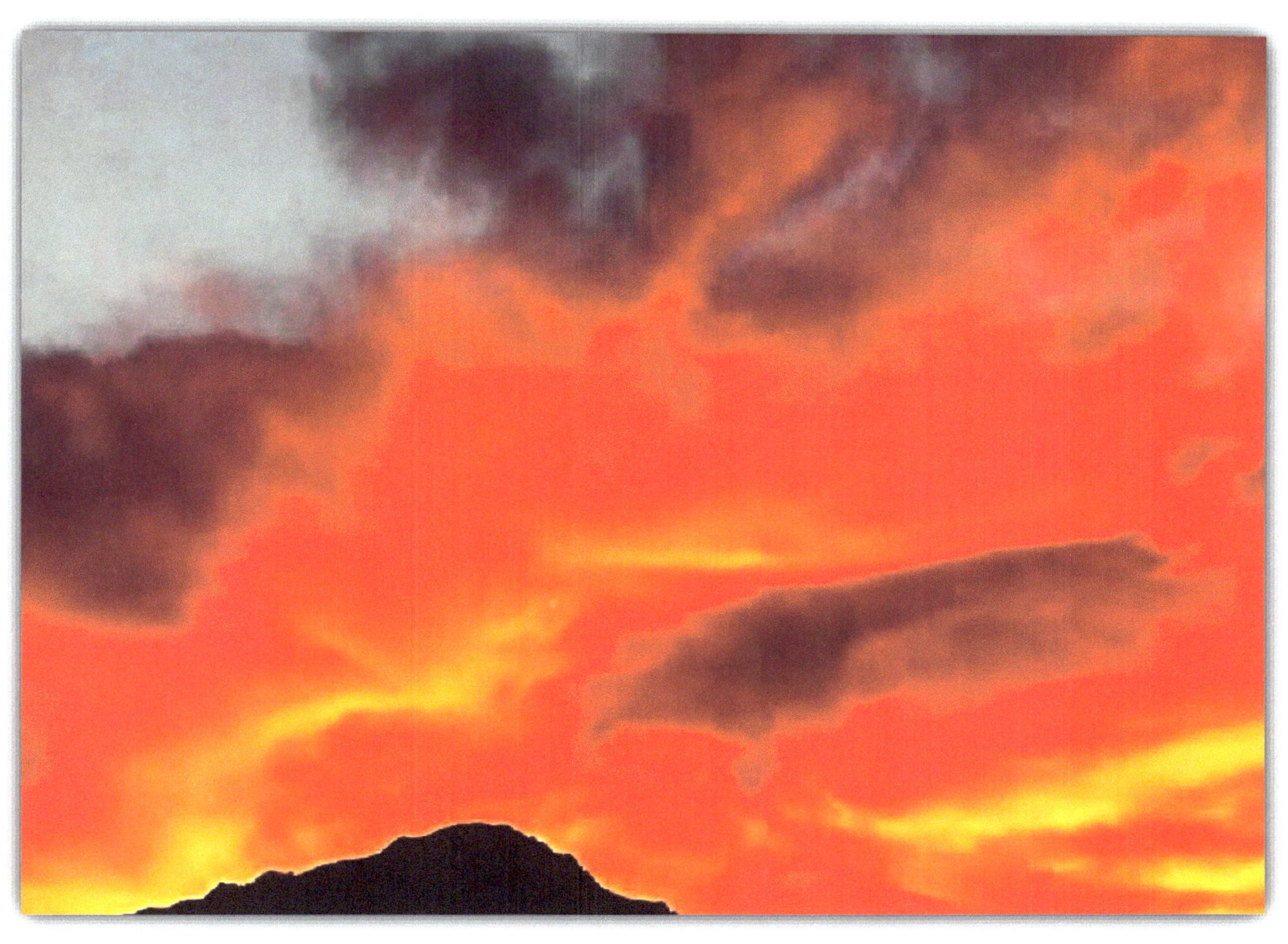

*Colorado skies will rarely fail to delight those who
pause to watch at dusk.*

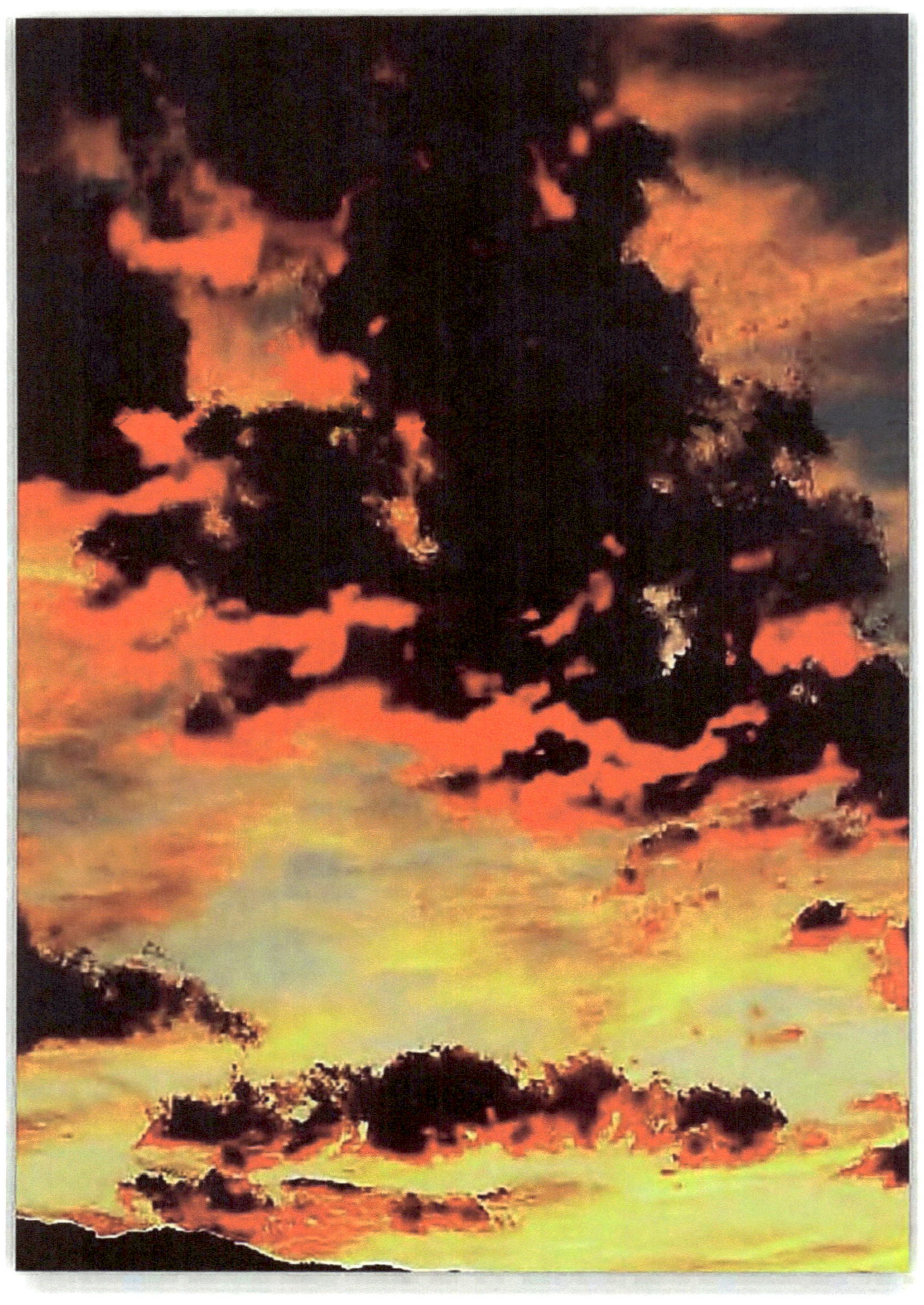

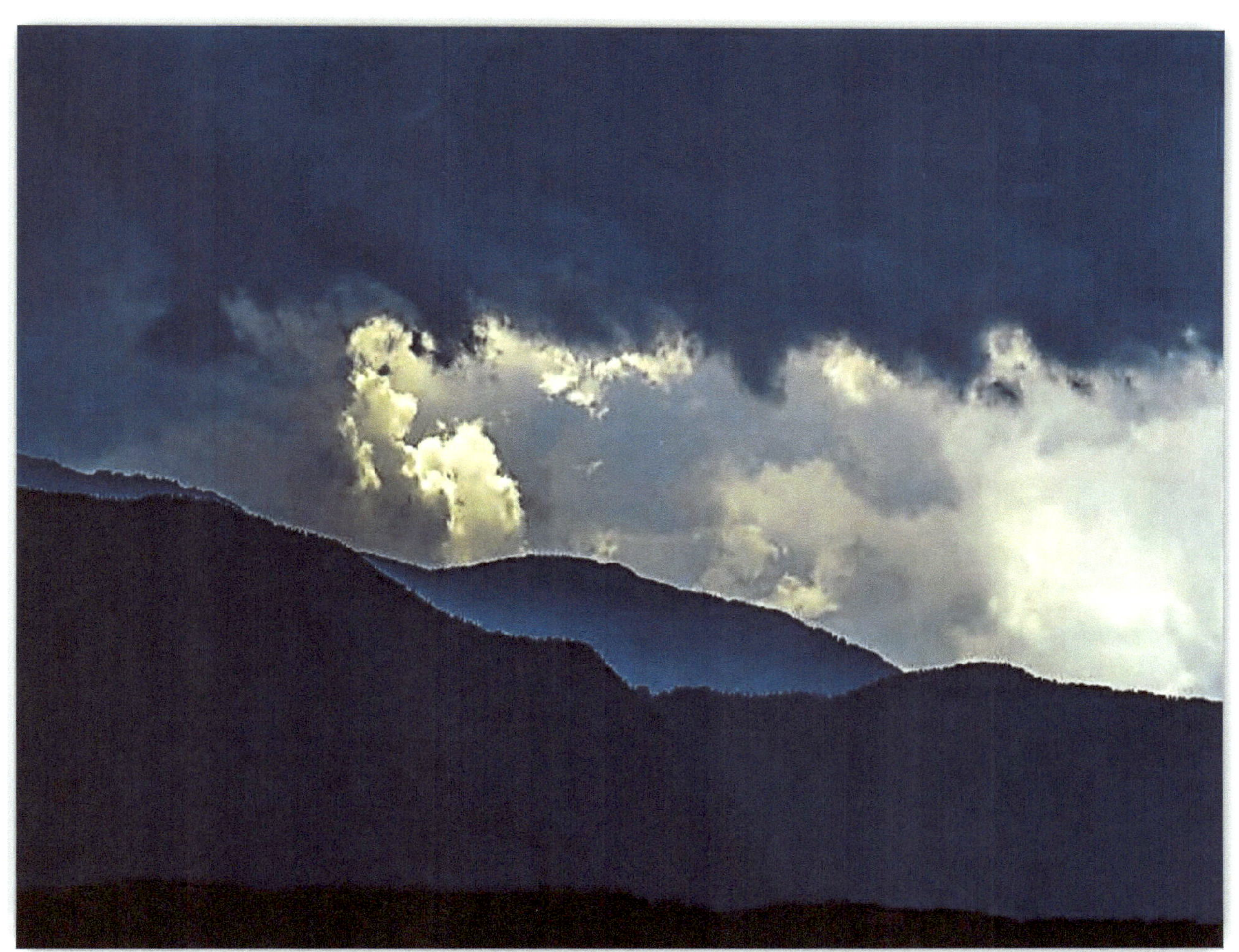

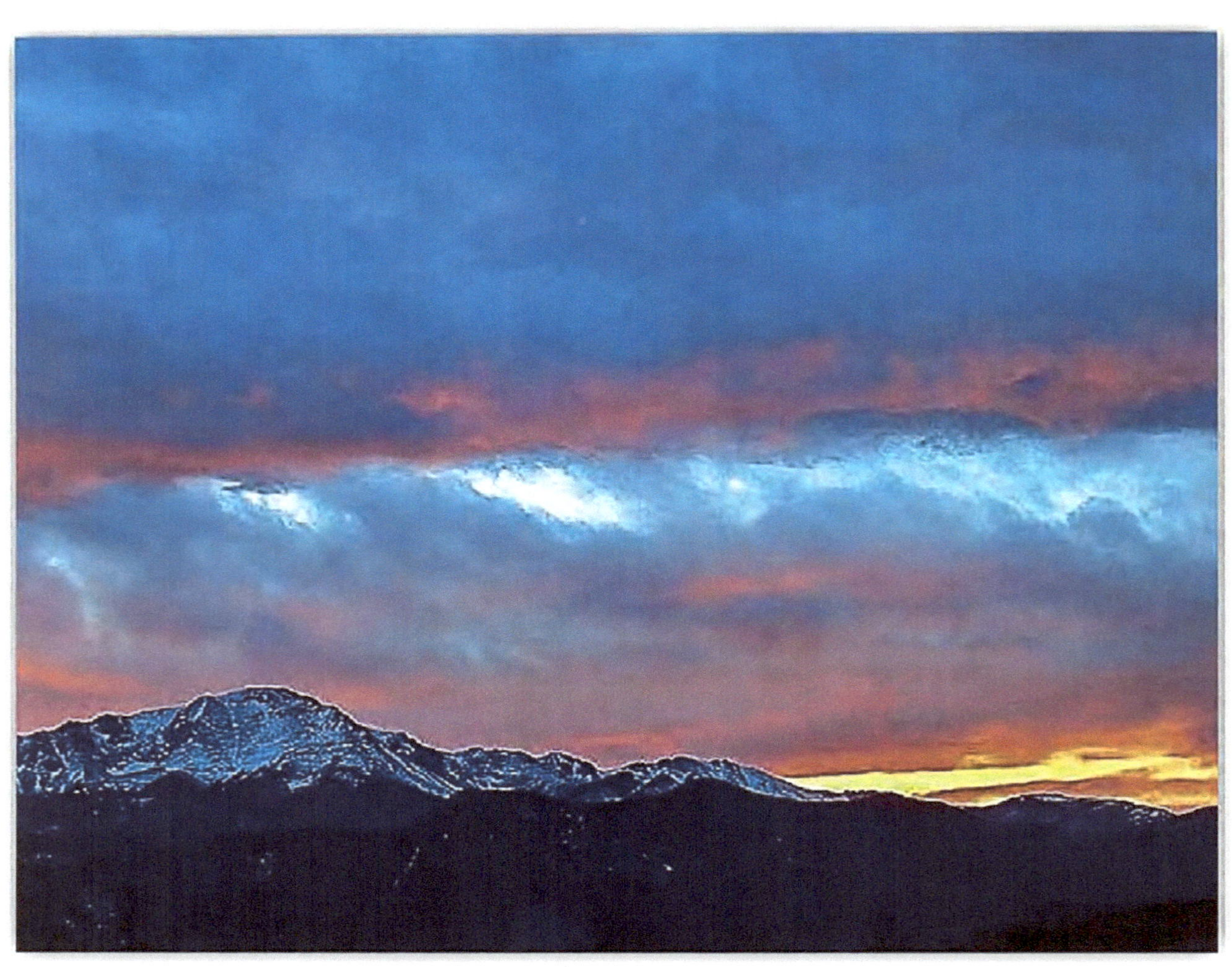

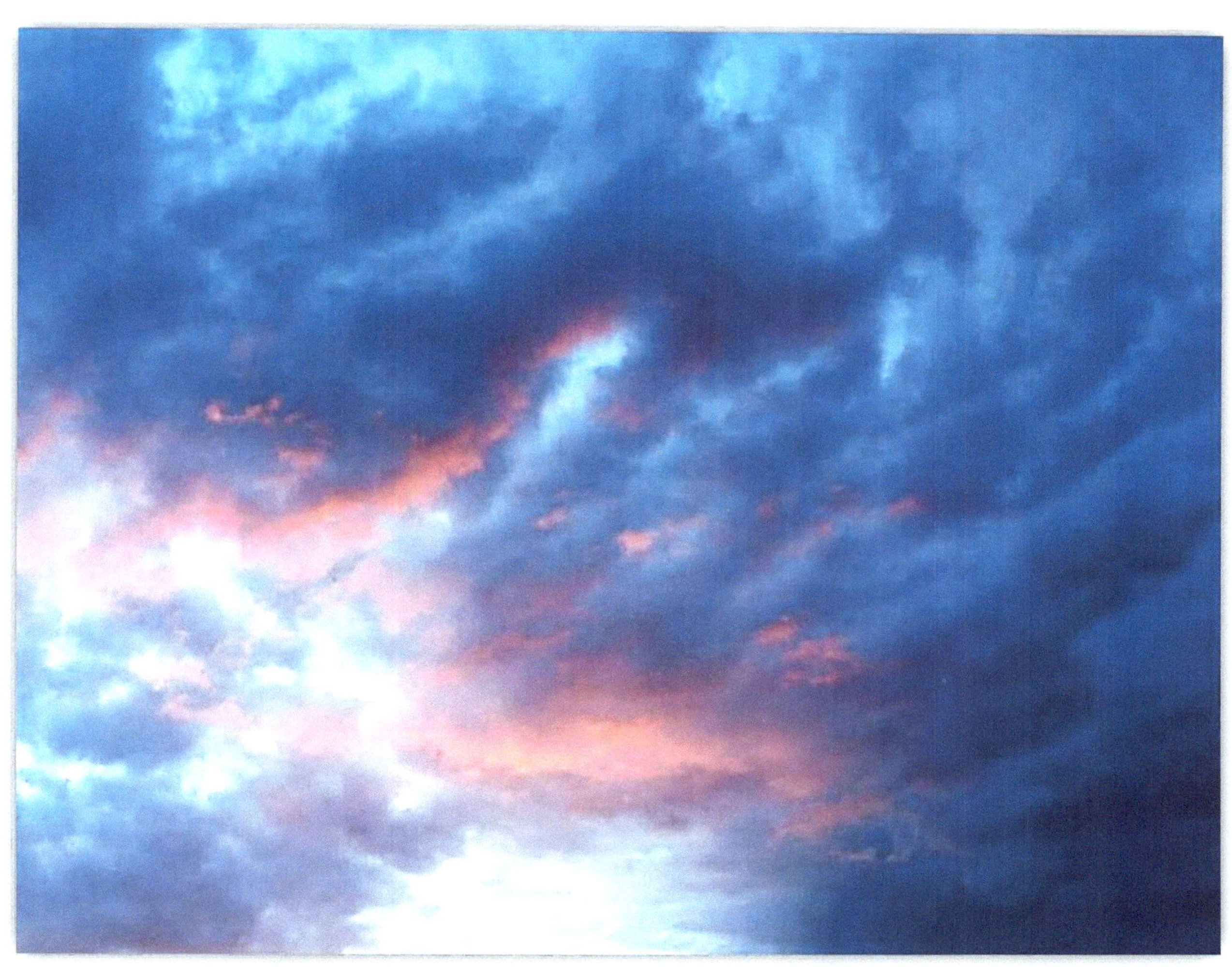

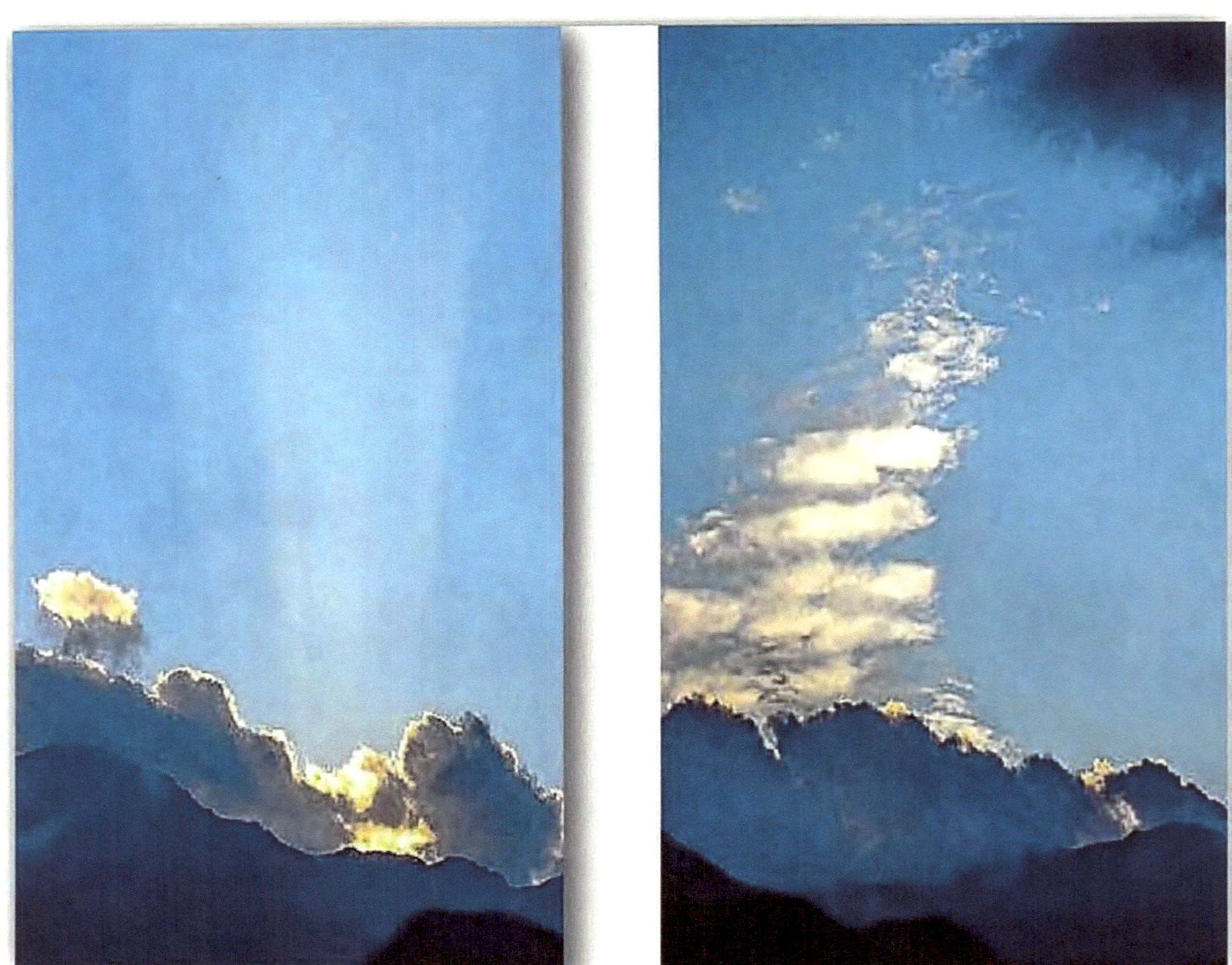

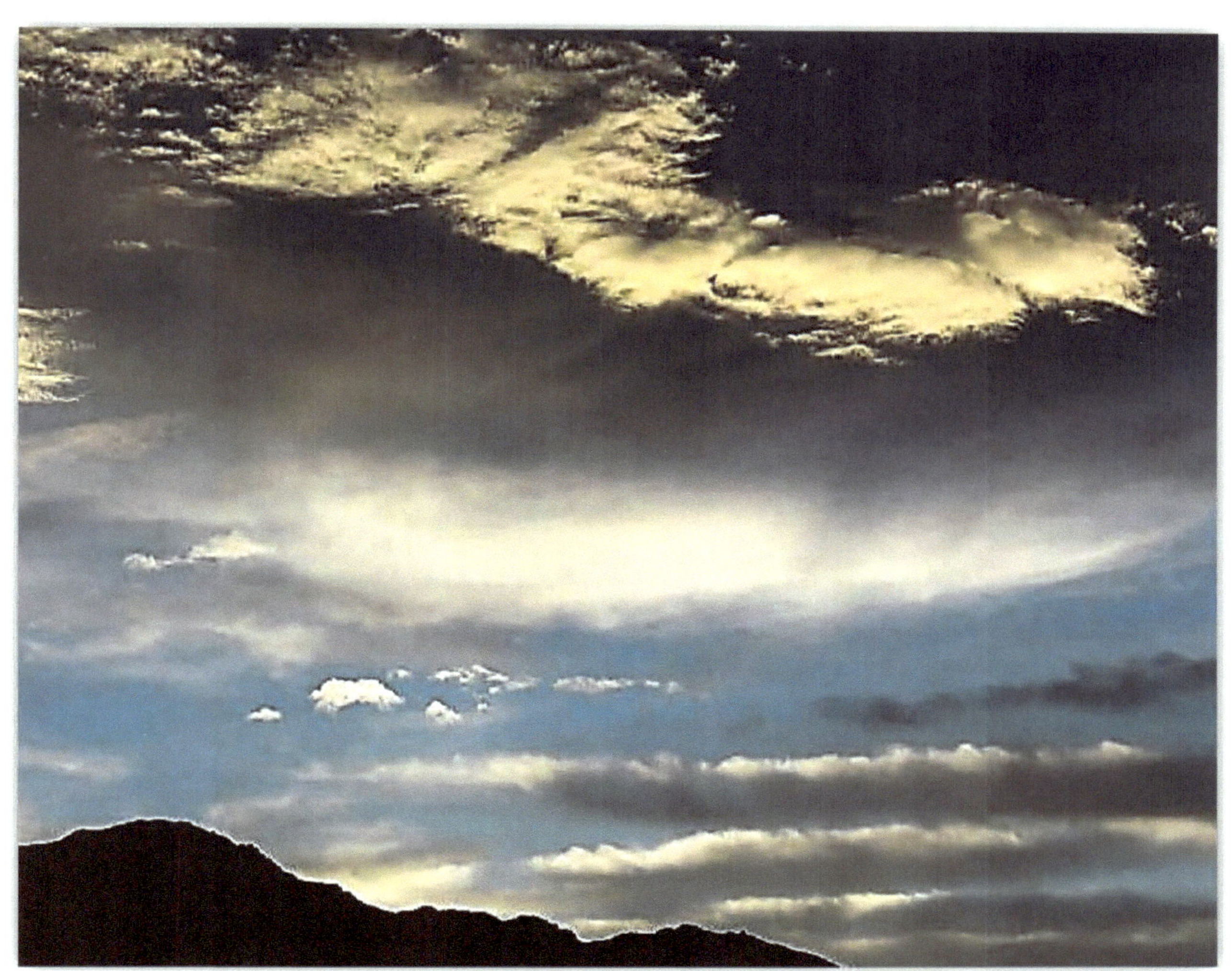

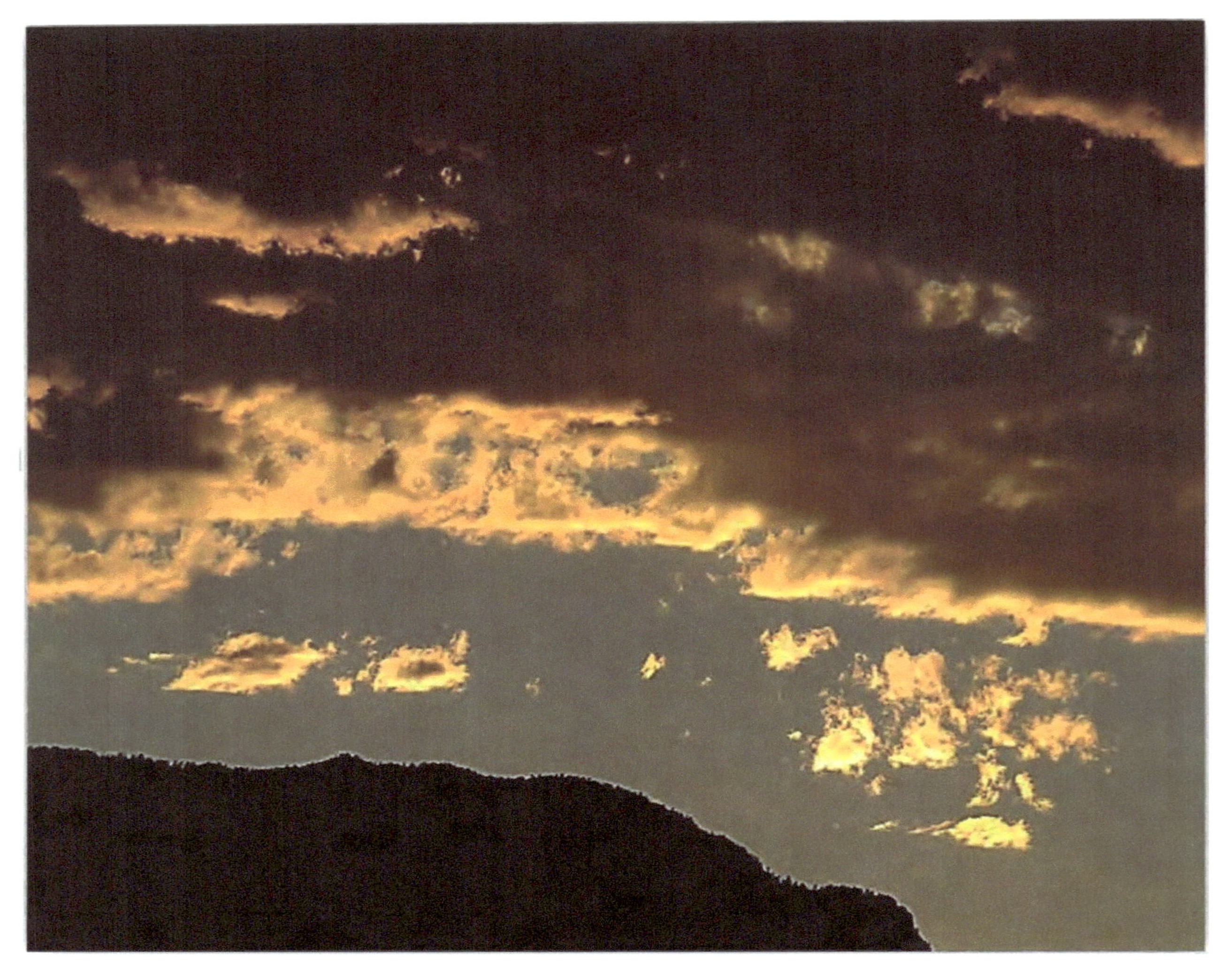

I think "Pikes Peak-or-Bust"
should be on the bucket list of
every lover of scenic skies.

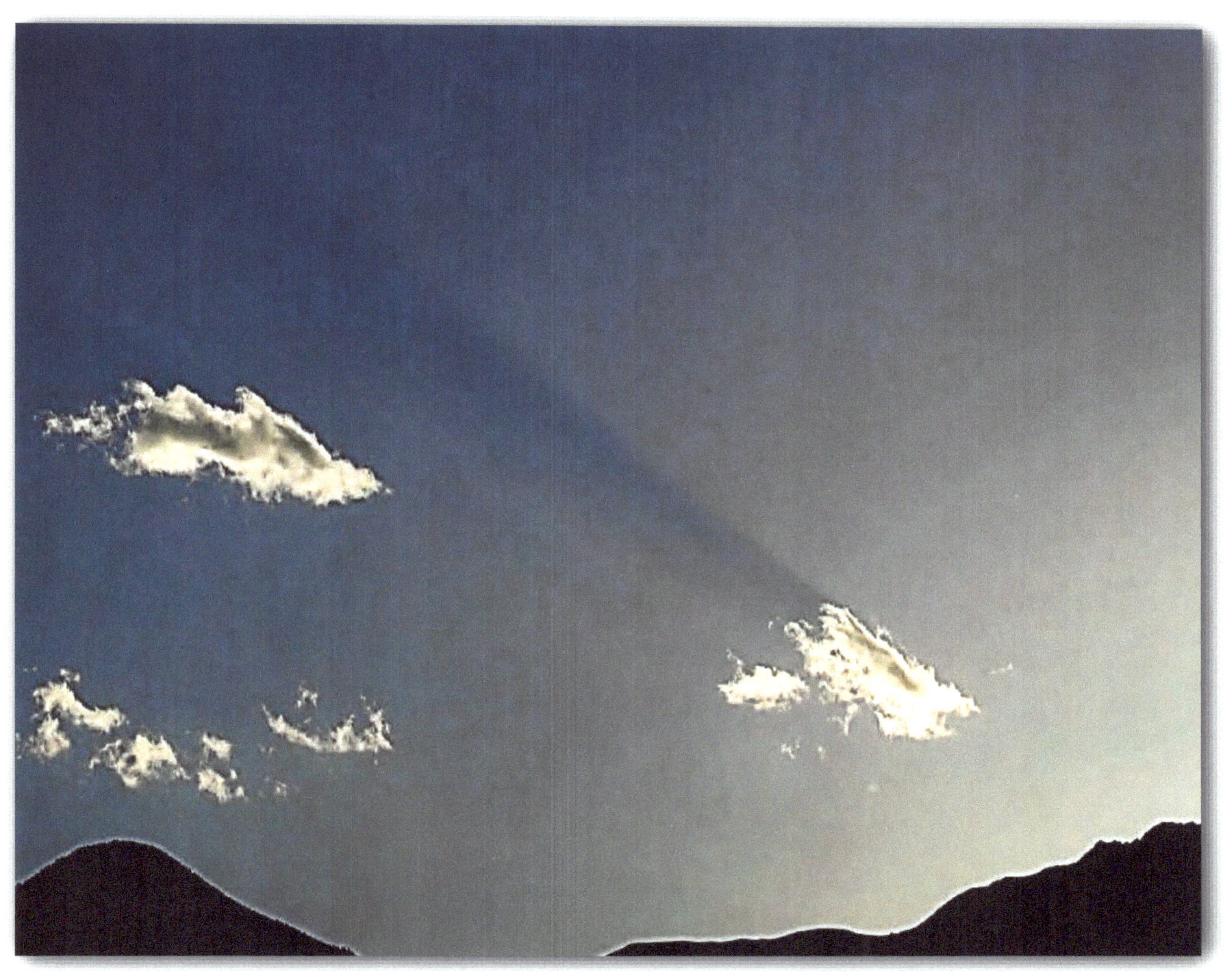

Wow!

Dear Friends,
I am pleased to proffer two original book series:

Books Designed with Leisure in Mind

These full-color photo essays
provide calming entertainment during times of waiting.
Perfect for living room or office.

Sleeping Moose Saga

A creative nonfiction-narrative ,the Sleeping Moose
set is a sharing of adventures my parents experienced
through a dozen years of pioneering on the Last Frontier.
The trilogy recounts my mom's tales of life as a pioneer in
the last decades before PCs or four-wheelers,
cellphones or solar panels, or any other kind of
silicon-chip technology had been heard of.
Those things probably would have made off-grid living
a little easier, but Dad still says
this was the highlight of his life.
And my mother admits that she liked parts of it, too.

These books can be purchased POD at

Amazonbooks:atwood cutting

Bulk orders through **Ingramcontent.com**

Thank you, and I wish each of you good health. A.C.

Books Designed with Leisure in Mind

<u>Yuri Yawns</u> (A short story for children and cat people.)
<u>Rural Missouri in the Fall</u> (Colors abound in a Midwest autumn.)
<u>Destination:Pikes Peak</u> (Is "Pikes Peak-or-Bust" on your Bucket List?)
<u>Our Lovely Autumn Drive</u> (Colorado to Oregon and back.)
<u>A Visit to the "North Forty"</u> (A little spot in Central California.)
<u>Winter Butterflies</u> (Imagination is a good starting place for stories.)
<u>A Day in NYC</u>(Country girl visits the Big Apple.)
<u>Riding a Zephyr into the Past</u> (Amtrak to Sacramento.)
<u>Chandeliers and Round Things</u> (Youngsters can identify objects.)
<u>Iris Impressions from Atwood</u> (A lover of "the poor man's orchid.")
<u>Dawn & Dusk</u> (Could the sky be any more beautiful?)
<u>Moonstruck</u> (Casual perspectives of our moon.)
<u>Clouds for Barbara</u> (Denizens floating over our heads.)
<u>Our 20th Century Wilderness Adventure</u> (Family life in "bush" Alaska.)

Sleeping Moose Saga (Memoir of a pioneer woman.)

Part 1: <u>Where the Moose Slept</u> (Newlyweds off to "See the Elephant.")
Part 2: <u>The Winter of '79</u> (Journals of a Wilderness Wife.)
Part 3: <u>Elephant in the Bush</u> (Maybe Emerson was mistaken.)

My mother, Kate, told me these true stories, and I wrote them down for you. Mom was from Hawaii, and Dad was from Boston. It's pretty amazing that they met in Alaska and shared a common yen to build a log cabin in the woods. Together they worked in a Trans-Alaska Pipeline construction camp, then took their grub-steak, and headed south, looking for the place they would call home. They found it on the Kenai.

Large print makes this saga a pleasant read for all ages. And more than two hundred black/white photos taken during twelve years of coping with whatever Alaska threw their way will surely bring these tales to life. (The trilogy is available in both paperback and ebook.)

www.ingramcontent.com/pod-product-compliance
Lightning Source LLC
Chambersburg PA
CBHW042153030726
47599CB00004B/715